CREATING YOUR

High School Resume

A Step-by-Step Guide to Preparing an Effective Resume for College, Training, and Jobs

THIRD EDITION

Kathryn Kraemer Troutman

jist Works
America's Career Publisher®

Creating Your High School Resume, Third Edition

© 2009 by Kathryn Kraemer Troutman

Published by JIST Works, an imprint of JIST Publishing
875 Montreal Way
St. Paul, MN 55102
E-mail: info@jist.com   Web site: www.jist.com

> **Note to instructors:** This workbook is part of a curriculum that also includes a portfolio workbook
> (*Creating Your High School Portfolio,* ISBN 978-1-59357-665-3) and an instructor's guide. Instructor's
> guides for both books are available on CD-ROM. The workbooks can be used separately or together,
> depending on your class objectives. All materials are available separately from JIST.

Keynote Speaker: Teachers and students, please feel free to contact Kathryn Troutman at kathryn@resume-place.
com for information about high school resume workshops for teachers and educators and conference presentations.

Workbook Product Manager: Lori Cates Hand
Development Editor: Aaron Black
Cover and Interior Designer: Aleata Halbig
Cover Photo: PhotoDisc
Proofreader: Jeanne Clark
Indexer: Jeanne Clark

Printed in the United States of America

19 18 17 16 15 14   12 11 10 9 8 7

ISBN: 978-1-59357-662-2

Contents

Foreword

So much of one's personal success depends on being aware of one's strengths and being prepared to use them in an appropriate way. *Creating Your High School Resume* recognizes that students in high school need the tools to discover their own identity and career path. It also acknowledges the importance of excellence in preparing top-quality presentations of oneself in resumes, cover letters, and interviews.

The tenth-grade students in the Civic Leadership Program of the Glenelg Country School in Howard County, Maryland, have benefited greatly from the introspective exercises, resume models, and suggestions for promoting excellence in personal presentation found in previous editions of *Creating Your High School Resume.* I am pleased to have collaborated with Kathryn Kraemer Troutman on this new edition to make it even more valuable for high school students.

Using this book as a reference guide for interview preparation, resume development, cover letter writing, and networking will help students position themselves for success in the college admissions process and in the workplace. With these arenas of development on one's career path becoming increasingly competitive, it is essential to take advantage of resources such as this book.

David C. Weeks, Director
Civic Leadership and Community Service Programs
Glenelg Country School, Howard County, Maryland

About This Book and CD-ROM

This will probably be your first resume and first resume book. At this point you can use a resume for getting a summer or part-time job, for college applications, to apply for internships, or simply to complete your homework for a high school class. This will be the easiest resume you will ever write.

The high school student samples in this book are from all kinds of students who are juniors and seniors. Look at the samples to get ideas about how to write about your high school activities (such as sports, theater, and student government), course descriptions, internships, and jobs.

Check out the keyword sections in chapter 3 so that you can begin to recognize keywords in your experiences and competencies and use them on your resume. Keywords are words that describe your skills. Examples of keywords could be *computer skills, creativity, detail-oriented,* or *organized.*

Creating Your High School Resume is a unique workbook that takes you step-by-step through the resume writing process. The CD-ROM in the back of the book provides resume samples in Microsoft Word format that you can use as templates to type over and use for your own resume content. Using a resume template can help you build your own resume faster.

Acknowledgments

Staying inspired and in touch with high school students and resume writing takes staying in touch with teachers. I want to thank David Weeks from Glenelg Country School in Columbia, Maryland, for going through the entire book to review usable and new ideas for this third edition. He uses the book in his Community Service courses every year, and his ideas run throughout the book. Also, a special thank you to Trish Snyder, who is a high school Navy recruitment manager and has provided insight into the high school resume for military officer training and scholarships. The Resume Place, Inc., Certified Professional Resume Writers provided resumes and stories for case studies for its high school and college students. Martha Raver, an accomplished athlete, provided her high school resume. Stephen Moffitt provided research for high school student Web sites, keywords, and internship opportunities. Craig Taylor helped organize the 30+ samples for this book and CD-ROM.

I'd also like to thank Aaron Black and Lori Cates Hand for their editorial support in the creation of this new edition. The editors work very hard to clarify many resume samples, stories, insights, and lessons. This is a complex book to publish and make simple and easy to read! Thank you to everyone for your help and samples.

High school student case studies and samples were provided by the following professional resume writers:

Sharon M. Bowden, CPRW, CEIP
SMB Solutions
Atlanta, GA
Phone: (404) 264-1855
Fax: (404) 264-0592
E-mail: Sharon@startsavvy.com
www.startsavvy.com

Diane Burns, CPRW, CPCC, FJSTC, CCM, CCMC, CEIP, IJCTC, CLTMC
Career Marketing Techniques
Boise, ID area
Phone: (208) 323-9636
E-mail: dianecprw@aol.com
www.polishedresumes.com

Jessica Coffey, M.Ed., CPRW, CFRWC
The Resume Place, Inc.
jessica@resume-place.com
www.resume-place.com

Janet M. Ruck, MA, MBA, JCTC
Career Consultant
Columbia, MD
Phone: (410) 992-7917
E-mail: janetruck@yahoo.com

Nancy Segal, CFRW, CFJST
The Resume Place, Inc.
Evanston, IL
nancy@resume-place.com
Phone: (847) 866-6675

Trish Snyder, M.Ed.
Naval Academy BGO and Scholarships Advisor
Navy Recruiting Education Services
Millington, TN
Phone: (901) 581-9747
E-mail: trishsnyd@gmail.com

Emily K. Troutman, MPP
Writer & Photographer
Washington, DC
E-mail: troutman.emily@gmail.com

Carla M. Waskiewicz, CPRW, CFRWC
The Resume Place, Inc.
89 Mellor Ave.
Baltimore, MD 21228
Phone: (410) 744-4324
E-mail: carla@resume-place.com

David C. Weeks, Director
Civic Leadership and Community Service Programs
Glenelg Country School
12793 Folly Quarter Rd.
Ellicott City, MD 21042
Office: (410) 531-8600 x2411
E-mail: Weeks@glenelg.org
Web site: www.glenelg.org

Introduction

Creating Your High School Resume and its accompanying CD-ROM will be your job search guide through high school and as you enter college. Everything you need to know about resumes, cover letters, interview preparation, networking, important job and internship Web sites, and keywords is in this book for your use in building the best possible resume for many purposes.

- In chapter 1, you will see seven different kinds of resumes for various purposes: General, Job, Internship, Work-Study, Volunteer, Summer Workshop Program, and Military Scholarship applications.

- Chapter 2 is all about skills: soft skills and hard skills. You do have skills that you have developed during high school. Think about what they are and add them to your resume.

- Chapter 3 covers two formats of resumes: chronological and targeted. The targeted format is more creative, and you can use it for special objectives. Also, this chapter introduces keywords from job ads that you can use in your resume.

- Chapter 4 introduces how to write each section of your resume and gives you examples of what to include.

- Chapter 5 introduces two resume formats: paper and electronic. Many applications and resumes are online, but some are still sent by mail or as attached files in e-mails.

- Chapter 6 includes case studies of high school students who are seeking various college majors or internships. Each case study includes a sample resume and the story behind it.

- Chapter 7 includes other application elements, including cover letters, job application forms, questionnaires, reference lists, and thank-you notes.

- Chapter 8 discusses the important differences between a job and an internship and goes over networking to meet people who can lead you to jobs and internships. This also includes the most popular Web sites for finding high school jobs and internships. It also includes interview practice questions for jobs, internships, and college recruiters.

Congratulations on deciding to complete this workbook. Your preparation greatly increases your chances of finding success in your life and career!

Knowing What a Resume Is and Why You Need One

This chapter explains what a resume is and how you can use it to help you reach your educational and career goals after high school. It includes sample resumes for getting jobs, landing internships, applying for college, and more.

What Is a Resume?

A resume is a one-page summary of your high school education, activities, volunteer and paid experience, and skills. Whether you are writing a resume as a class assignment, actually looking for a job or internship, or applying for college, this will be the first of many resumes that you will write in your life.

Start a resume in ninth grade. Each semester or each year, you can add to and update it with your most recent achievements. As time goes on, you will have a very well-thought-out document that reflects a well-rounded individual.

Why a Resume Is So Important

A resume can help you

- Complete your class assignment.
- Land an internship, co-op, or work-study opportunity.
- Get into college and get a scholarship.
- Get a job.
- Keep track of your education, special courses, projects, and activities.
- Record your paid and unpaid work experience.
- Recognize your skills, interests, and accomplishments.

- Impress college recruiters and scholarship panels.
- Feel good about yourself and what you have done.

> **Tip** You might want to update your resume at least once a year throughout high school and beyond. You can easily revise your resume as you add jobs, skills, courses, honors, internships, and activities. This way, the resume will be ready if someone asks for it, or if you see an internship or a job that you're interested in.

High School Job Opportunities and Resumes Are Not All the Same

There are many opportunities for work, internships, training, and community service during your last two years of high school and following graduation.

This chapter includes samples of resumes for different purposes. Each resume contains the basic resume information, but they are individually focused by listing additional specific skills, experience, courses, and interests that would help a candidate stand out in the given focus area.

The resume formats and career ideas covered in this book are the following:

- **Basic Student Resume:** A beginner resume for your class that you can expand, develop, focus, and change depending on your objectives.

- **Internship Resume:** A resume that is focused toward the internship program, specialized experience, and mission of the organization you want to intern with. Internships can be either paid or unpaid.

- **College and College Scholarship Resume:** A resume that you can send with your college application and use to apply for scholarships based on performance, grades, and experience. This type of resume could pay off big in the form of scholarship dollars.

- **Job, Work-Study, or Co-op Resume:** A resume that will help you get a job or enter a work-study or co-op program. This resume presents the best employment and job skills you have to offer. Jobs and work-study and co-op positions are usually paid.

- **Summer Workshop Program Resume:** A resume targeted for summer programs that focus on special skills such as writing, theater, musical performance, sports, or arts. You can feature education, experience, or interests, depending on the program subject. Usually you pay to participate in these programs.

- **Community and Volunteer Service Resume:** A resume that focuses on skills that will be of interest to a community service or volunteer program. It should include or feature volunteer work and is useful for documenting required community service hours. Volunteer positions are usually unpaid.

- **Military Academy and Scholarship Resume:** A resume that features ROTC experience, leadership, discipline, teamwork, sports, grades, and other skills of interest to the U.S. military services. You can also use this type of resume with scholarship requests for help with tuition, books, and other reimbursements.

- **National Community Service Resume:** A resume targeted at competitive state and national programs for community service that give you human and social services experience. Some of these programs pay or offer living accommodations. Your community service resume will be impressive for college applications or applying for jobs.

The Basic Student Resume

The basic student resume is a beginner resume that can be expanded, developed, focused, and changed depending on your objectives. This resume should contain the outline of your education and experience. Major headings include the following:

- Personal information
- Education, including courses, activities, and awards
- Work experience
- Community service/volunteer activities and jobs

Use the following worksheet to review exactly how you want your personal information to look on your resume.

Personal Information Worksheet

List your pertinent personal information on the following lines. Be sure to include everything relevant. Think about how the information you provide here will influence an employer's view of you. Is your e-mail address appropriate? What phone number can you be reached at best (your cell might be better than your home)? Is your name easy to pronounce as is, or do you need to add a helpful note to explain the pronunciation?

_____

_____

_____

The following example is a resume with no information filled in. It shows you the pattern a basic resume should follow and what necessary information should be included.

NAME

Street Address
City, State, ZIP
Telephone
E-mail

Career Objective	Information stated as a goal statement
Education	Name of High School College Preparatory Program—Class of 20xx Summer Institute or School
Honors & Awards	Effort Honor Roll/Honor Roll/High Honor Roll—20xx–20xx Student Council Community Service Awards Volunteer Certification, 20xx
Experience	Experience number 1 Experience number 2 Experience number 3 Experience number 4
Extracurricular Activities	School Athletic Team *Level of athletic achievement, 20xx–20xx Club Membership, 20xx–20xx
Interests	Hobbies Relevant activities outside school
Personal References	Name (Relationship) Name (Relationship) Address Address Telephone Telephone

Later in this workbook you will work through a series of exercises to help you gather all of this information.

The following is an example of a basic resume. Review it to understand better how the preceding example looks with "real" information in it.

Ronald Williams

1010 Westminster Way
Chesterfield, VA 55555
(703) 777-7777
rwilliams@hotmail.com

Objective

My main goal is to gain business experience and education applicable to becoming a restaurant owner.

Education

Matoaca High School, Junior, expect to graduate June 20xx
Chesterfield, VA
Standard Diploma with Business Courses

Awards

Distinguished Honor Roll, 20xx–20xx

Work Experience

Chekmarc's Restaurant, May 20xx–May 20xx   Palm Bay, FL
Bus Boy, Dishwasher

Clear and clean tables. Greet customers. Wash dishes. Dependable and fast, and followed sanitation rules.

Skills

- Communications Skills (Oral, Written)
- Computer Skills (Microsoft Office)
- Customer Service Skills
- Organization Skills
- Time Management Skills

Hobbies

Sports, working out, spending time with family, traveling

Internship Resumes

Many corporations, small businesses, and government agencies offer 6- to 12-week summer internships or year-round internships with flexible hours to students who are 16 years or older, are enrolled in high school full time, and have GPAs of 2.5 or higher.

Some internship opportunities are paid; however, others are unpaid. An internship can give you hands-on experience in a certain industry that you might be interested in pursuing for a career or studying in college.

Internships on resumes look impressive to college recruiters, scholarship panels, and future employers.

The Application Process Can Be Complicated

The application process is actually a test to see whether you can follow directions and display professional mannerisms. You might find an online application to complete, which will include essays and questionnaires about your experience and interest in the career field. You might need to provide reference names or letters, your resume, and maybe a cover letter. You will have to work hard at completing the application. This is your first hurdle toward landing the internship.

The following example shows what an internship announcement might look like (this one is from Southwest Airlines). You will have to read an announcement well to fill out an application effectively. This announcement is loaded with keywords and pointers that will guide you toward what the employer will be looking for on the application.

Time Commitment:
- Full-time minimum 40 hours per week (Monday–Friday)

Pay:
- $9.00 per hour

Education:
- Major in an aviation/aeronautical-based undergraduate degree program
- Minimum sophomore level
- Student must have an additional semester of classes remaining after completion of the internship
- Maintained 2.5 or above GPA

Experience:
- Participation in organizations and clubs desirable
- Proficient with Microsoft Office applications
- Database applications helpful, but not required

Skills and Abilities:
- Excellent communication (reading and writing), analytical and organizational skills
- Ability to manage time and multiple tasks effectively
- FAA Flight Certificates and ratings desirable

Personal Traits:
- Customer service oriented
- Self-motivated and energetic
- Team oriented
- Ability to work equally well alone or with others
- Flexibility to work in a dynamic, fast-paced environment
- Sense of humor

Job Duties:
- Projects include research, presentation, and meeting or involvement with or for Engineering, Hotels, Safety, Training, Dispatch, Scheduling, ATC, Navigation, or Chief Pilots (varies each term).

How to Submit an Application

All internship positions are located in Dallas, TX, at Southwest Airlines Headquarters. In order to apply, you must U.S. mail the following information:

- Cover letter
- Resume
- Unofficial transcript
- Essay "Why Southwest Airlines?"
  Length is up to the author
- Letters of Recommendation (If you have any.)
- Flight & Medical Certificates (If you have any.)

People Department, College Coordinator, Southwest Airlines

PO Box 36611, HDQ 4HR, Dallas, TX 75235

Resume Keywords Worksheet

Review the preceding announcement sample and write on the following lines which keywords and phrases you think you would need to include on an application for this position.

_____

_____

_____

Tips for High School Internship Resumes

In your resume for an internship, you should show that you are sincere, dependable, and interested in the organization. You should also describe your qualifications and explain why you are applying. You must show that you are worthy of a company's time and training.

The following is a sample resume in response to the application you just looked at. Notice that this resume directly responds to the ad and what the airline is looking for.

CALVIN KLINE

2501B WHEATON WAY
DAVIS, CALIFORNIA 00000
(970) 000-0000

ACADEMIC GOAL:

To complete my A.S. degree in Business Administration and obtain an internship in Commercial Aeronautics Program.

CAREER GOAL:

To gain relevant work experience using my education, prior experience, and strong technical skills toward my goal of becoming a commercial airline pilot.

SKILLS SUMMARY:

Excellent mechanical skills   Welcome challenging projects
Detail-oriented and responsible   Strong technical and diagnostic skills
        Enjoy hands-on technical projects and automotive repair/restoration

EDUCATION:

La Quinta High School, Davis, CA Class of 20xx

Completed Technical Program, focusing on Industrial Design and Automotive Diagnostics and Repair. **Courses included:** Industrial Physics, Welding, Machining, Drafting, Automotive Drive Train/Heating/AC, and Diagnostics and Electrical. **GPA 4.0 in all technical courses.**

Proven technical capabilities!

Honors & Awards:
- Merit Awards in Welding and Automotive.
- **Received three-year full scholarship** to attend Community College of South California.
- Accepted into Commercial Aeronautics Program, AIMS Community College, Foresman, California. Expect to graduate in 20xx.

Proven responsible work experience

EMPLOYMENT:

Auto Technician	HIGHLINE MOTORS, Davis, CA - Summer 20xx Repair and maintain high-end import cars.
Installer	VANWORKS, Greeley, CA - Summer 20xx Installed leather interiors, running boards, custom electronics, and aftermarket accessories for this custom conversion van company.
Craftsman	WOOD SHOP, Mead, CA - Summer 20xx Crafted custom dashboards from quality hardwoods and veneers.
Autotech Trainee	WILF'S EUROPEAN MOTORS, Mead, CA - Summer 20xx

SPORTS / SPECIAL INTERESTS:

Purchase, repair, and sell custom-built automobiles. Projects completed include a 1977 Porsche 930 and a 1976 FJ40 Four Wheeler - rebuilt and restored from the frame up.
Compete in local auto races. Collect and ride dirt bikes.
Won People's Choice Award in local 4x4 show for 1978 Chevy Truck.
High School sports included boxing and swim team.

Shows passion, quality work, and dedication

Recommendations: Upon request

Job, Work-Study, Internship, and Co-op Resumes

A good resume makes looking for work much easier. Many employers are impressed by high school students with resumes. To apply for a job, you should e-mail, mail, or hand-deliver your resume and cover letter to the employer. Chapter 7 gives tips for writing a cover letter. Chapter 8 provides information about looking for a job.

Online Job Applications and Resumes

You can use several different methods to submit a resume. Many employers now ask that you send your resume by e-mail. You can also apply for jobs online by copying and pasting your resume into an online resume builder that the company supplies. And, of course, you can mail the resume. Use an envelope that's a little larger than your resume so that you do not have to fold your resume. The employer might want to scan it into a database, which will be difficult if it has been folded.

You should have a resume both on paper and in an electronic format. You'll see samples of both formats in this book.

Even if a company uses job applications, attach your resume to the application. This saves you time and will impress the person who reviews the application. Keep your jobs, courses, and references up-to-date. Some employers won't accept a resume in place of an application, but will probably accept the resume in addition to the application.

Be ready with a resume all the time. You never know when you will meet someone who can help you get a job. Many employers are looking for hardworking students. You might get job information from your parents, friends of your parents, your friends' parents, business owners, and local businesses. A resume is the icing on the cake. These people might already think you'd be a good worker, but your resume pulls everything together and proves that you are!

The following resume is by a student interested in an internship in the field of cosmetics.

Gloria Ramirez

101 Edmondson Avenue
Springfield, IL 66666
(555) 555-3333
g_ramirez@yahoo.com

Education

Springfield High School, Springfield, IL
Junior; expect to graduate May 20xx
Honor Roll, 20xx–20xx

Activities demonstrate interest in business and leadership skills

Activities

Sophomore Class Vice President—School Year 20xx–20xx
Lead meetings, planned events, planned fund-raising.

Member of Future Business Leaders of America—School Year 20xx–20xx

Freshman Class Treasurer—School Year 20xx–20xx
Handled budgets, fund-raising, and cash control.

Cosmetics Internship *Focused experience is great!*
Two-month internship with training for Merle Norman Cosmetics—20xx

Hard and soft skills

Skills Summary
Leadership and organizational skills
Customer service and public relations skills *These are keywords for Aveda*
Computer skills; Microsoft Office; keyboard 50 wpm *Always add keyboarding skills*
Bilingual: Spanish and English

Employment

The Perfect Touch, Springfield, IL (15 hours/week)—July 20xx–October 20xx
Retail Sales and Cosmetics Consultant for Merle Norman Cosmetics.
Assisted with product merchandising, inventory control, displays, and customer service. Advised customers in product selection and colors, and assisted with makeup services. Recognized for professionalism; customer care; and flexibility when working for special events, including weddings and proms.

Bagel Bin, Springfield, IL (15 hours/week)—March–June 20xx
Prepared sandwiches and operated cash register.

Excellent experience in a small shop with cosmetics

Applications can look complicated and scary. Remember, the job description will tell you what kind of person the employer is seeking. Find the important keywords to use or demonstrate on the application and in your resume.

Chapter 7 explores applications further. To get started with exploring the application process, try the following exercise.

Job Application Questions Exercise

The following is an ad for a barista position at a coffee house followed by several example application questions for the position. Try answering the questions using the ad as though you were interested in the position.

Job Ad

"Cool Beans Coffee is seeking a barista for its downtown Seattle location. Unlimited opportunity to advance. Qualified applicant will demonstrate a zealous love of coffee, a winning customer-focused personality, and a drive for success in a barista career."

Application Questions

Have you been a Cool Beans customer before? At which location? Tell us about your experience:

_____

_____

_____

Do you love coffee? Why?

_____

_____

_____

Why do you want to work for Cool Beans?

_____

_____

_____

Give an example of perfect customer service you have provided. What did you do so well in the situation?

_____

_____

_____

Special Summer Workshop Program Resumes

You might have to complete an application and personal statement to apply for summer programs. You can also enclose your one-page resume, which serves as a quick review for the admissions committee. A resume can set you apart from other applicants by showing that you are professional, sincere, and ready to go.

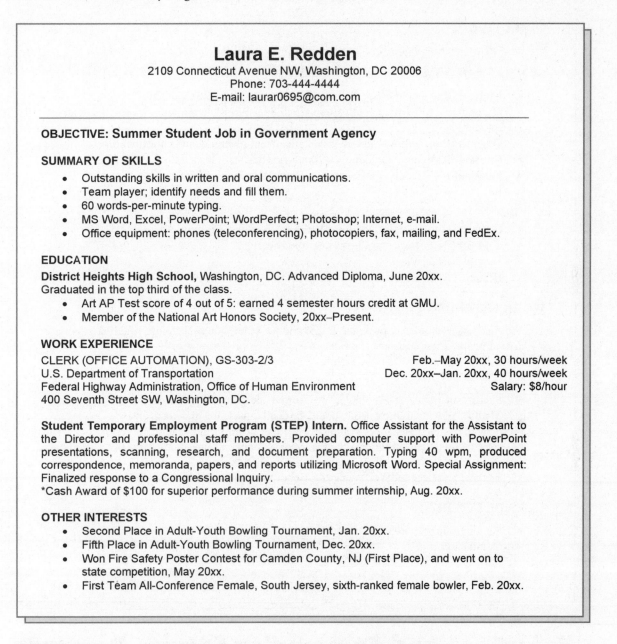

Laura E. Redden
2109 Connecticut Avenue NW, Washington, DC 20006
Phone: 703-444-4444
E-mail: laurar0695@com.com

OBJECTIVE: Summer Student Job in Government Agency

SUMMARY OF SKILLS

- Outstanding skills in written and oral communications.
- Team player; identify needs and fill them.
- 60 words-per-minute typing.
- MS Word, Excel, PowerPoint; WordPerfect; Photoshop; Internet, e-mail.
- Office equipment: phones (teleconferencing), photocopiers, fax, mailing, and FedEx.

EDUCATION

District Heights High School, Washington, DC. Advanced Diploma, June 20xx.
Graduated in the top third of the class.

- Art AP Test score of 4 out of 5: earned 4 semester hours credit at GMU.
- Member of the National Art Honors Society, 20xx–Present.

WORK EXPERIENCE

CLERK (OFFICE AUTOMATION), GS-303-2/3
U.S. Department of Transportation
Federal Highway Administration, Office of Human Environment
400 Seventh Street SW, Washington, DC.

Feb.–May 20xx, 30 hours/week
Dec. 20xx–Jan. 20xx, 40 hours/week
Salary: $8/hour

Student Temporary Employment Program (STEP) Intern. Office Assistant for the Assistant to the Director and professional staff members. Provided computer support with PowerPoint presentations, scanning, research, and document preparation. Typing 40 wpm, produced correspondence, memoranda, papers, and reports utilizing Microsoft Word. Special Assignment: Finalized response to a Congressional Inquiry.
*Cash Award of $100 for superior performance during summer internship, Aug. 20xx.

OTHER INTERESTS

- Second Place in Adult-Youth Bowling Tournament, Jan. 20xx.
- Fifth Place in Adult-Youth Bowling Tournament, Dec. 20xx.
- Won Fire Safety Poster Contest for Camden County, NJ (First Place), and went on to state competition, May 20xx.
- First Team All-Conference Female, South Jersey, sixth-ranked female bowler, Feb. 20xx.

Resumes for Work-Study or Co-op Programs

In a work-study or co-op program, you will spend part of your day taking regular courses and part of your day at a job. This experience gives you good exposure to the workplace before graduation. You are sometimes paid for work-study jobs. You will have a better chance of getting into a work-study or co-op program if you have a good resume. Following is an example.

Danielle N. Edgington
109 Colleen Road
Alexandria, Virginia 20165
(703) 888-0888
E-mail: danielle@yahoo.com

OBJECTIVE

Office position requiring computer, administrative, and customer service skills.

SUMMARY OF SKILLS

- **Clerical:** File maintenance, office administration, mail management
- **Computers:** MS Office applications (including Word), keyboard 55 wpm, data entry, Internet
- **Organization:** Follow-through on details, event planning, and coordination
- **Communications:** Telephone, customer service, team leadership
- **Personality:** Friendly, quick learner, dependable, hard worker

EDUCATION

- Calvary Temple School, Sterling, Virginia, Graduate Class of 20xx
- GPA 3.4
- Varsity Basketball
- Drama Teams

WORK EXPERIENCE

Various jobs as child care provider, house and pet sitter, house cleaning, wedding planner's assistant, and office assistant

VOLUNTEER WORK

- Facility maintenance—Volunteer worker on church and community beautification days. Member of team to provide lawn and garden landscaping and clean-up.
- Special events organizer—Volunteer coordinator for birthday and anniversary celebrations. Plan activities, schedule other volunteers, and organize events. Coordinated several events with more than 100 people in attendance.
- Teacher's assistant—Work with art teacher to manage children and activities.

OUTSIDE INTERESTS

- Youth group activities
- Youth choir

Volunteer and Community Service Resumes

Community service and volunteer work can give you qualifications, experience, and networks for your future career. Most high schools require students to perform volunteer and community service work to qualify for graduation. You can find out what opportunities are available by talking with your school guidance counselor and service-learning coordinator.

A volunteer or community service job can help you get a paid position in the same field. Select volunteer and community service positions carefully and look for work that uses your skills and interests. Apply with a resume so that the manager can see your skills and interests. Remember that the employer is giving you an opportunity to learn and gain a reference for future positions. The following sample resume was created for pursuing a volunteer position.

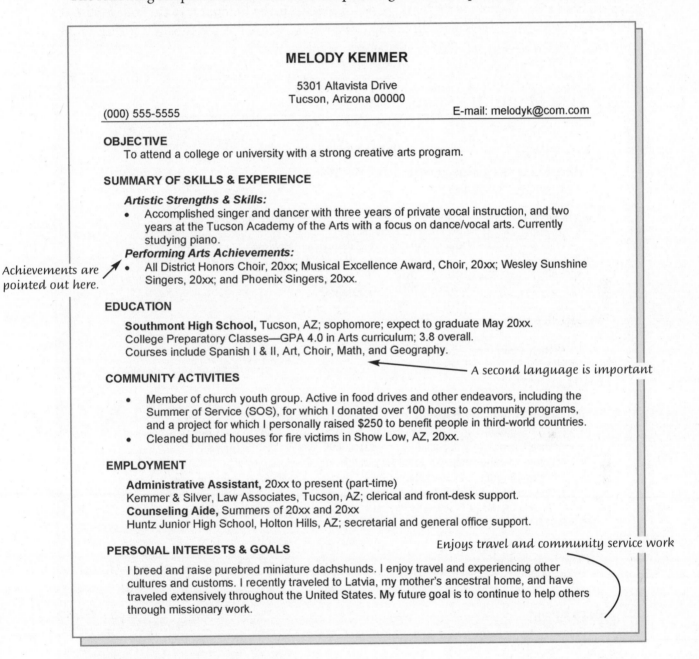

MELODY KEMMER

5301 Altavista Drive
Tucson, Arizona 00000

(000) 555-5555   E-mail: melodyk@com.com

OBJECTIVE
    To attend a college or university with a strong creative arts program.

SUMMARY OF SKILLS & EXPERIENCE

Artistic Strengths & Skills:
- Accomplished singer and dancer with three years of private vocal instruction, and two years at the Tucson Academy of the Arts with a focus on dance/vocal arts. Currently studying piano.

Performing Arts Achievements:
- All District Honors Choir, 20xx; Musical Excellence Award, Choir, 20xx; Wesley Sunshine Singers, 20xx; and Phoenix Singers, 20xx.

Achievements are pointed out here.

EDUCATION

Southmont High School, Tucson, AZ; sophomore; expect to graduate May 20xx.
College Preparatory Classes—GPA 4.0 in Arts curriculum; 3.8 overall.
Courses include Spanish I & II, Art, Choir, Math, and Geography.

A second language is important

COMMUNITY ACTIVITIES

- Member of church youth group. Active in food drives and other endeavors, including the Summer of Service (SOS), for which I donated over 100 hours to community programs, and a project for which I personally raised $250 to benefit people in third-world countries.
- Cleaned burned houses for fire victims in Show Low, AZ, 20xx.

EMPLOYMENT

Administrative Assistant, 20xx to present (part-time)
Kemmer & Silver, Law Associates, Tucson, AZ; clerical and front-desk support.
Counseling Aide, Summers of 20xx and 20xx
Huntz Junior High School, Holton Hills, AZ; secretarial and general office support.

Enjoys travel and community service work

PERSONAL INTERESTS & GOALS

I breed and raise purebred miniature dachshunds. I enjoy travel and experiencing other cultures and customs. I recently traveled to Latvia, my mother's ancestral home, and have traveled extensively throughout the United States. My future goal is to continue to help others through missionary work.

College Resumes

An up-to-date resume can help you with your college applications and the personal statement that many colleges require. When you have a record of your activities, honors, and courses, you can fill out the applications much faster. Include the resume with your package. It will help admissions representatives understand your background. It will also demonstrate your organizational skills.

Your resume can even help you write a college admissions essay. You can look at your resume and write about a significant educational experience that would be of interest to the college admissions representative. Following is an example of a resume written to accompany a college application.

KYLIE MARIE JENNINGS

124 Hana Avenue, Haiku, HI 99999 • (555) 555-9999
E-mail: bigwave@net.net

EDUCATION

HALL COLLEGE PREPARATORY, Olinda, Maui, Hawaii
Expect to graduate in 20xx

Academic Courses: Headmaster's List, GPA: 3.9 (20xx–20xx school year)
Japanese I and Spanish IV
Honors Physics, Pre-Calculus, and Spanish

Activities: Member, Cross-Country and Track Teams
Second in Maui County, 20xx

WORKSHOPS

Smyth School of Art, Washington, DC, summer 20xx—Studio Art and Photography
Costa Rica, Central America, summer 20xx—Spanish-Language Immersion

EMPLOYMENT

MAUI RETAIL CORP., Lahaina, Maui, 20xx–present
Retail Sales/Computer Assistant to the Regional Manager
- Perform computer research concerning inventory, costs, and store information.
- Research competitive companies, products, and catalogs via the Internet.
- Manipulate online data to create sales and financial reports.
- Develop formulas and create Excel spreadsheets, graphs, and reports for management and financial analysis by managers.
- Conducted retail sales, friendly customer service, inventory control, and merchandising.

SKILLS

Languages: Fluent Spanish; currently studying Japanese
Computers: PCs with Windows Vista, Excel, Word

INTERESTS

Extensive travel in the United States and Central America
Hawaiian culture and history
Philosophy and environmental sciences
Outdoor activities, including hiking, camping, and biking

PERSONAL QUALITIES

Dependable, hardworking, motivated, sincere, and analytical
Challenged by learning and new experiences

Applying for Scholarships

Many scholarship applications request work samples, personal statements, letters, and other information. Along with those materials, you can also enclose your resume to give the scholarship committee a total picture of your education and experience. You will save the committee time, create a good impression, and help the members make a decision about the scholarship.

Following is a resume written to accompany a scholarship application.

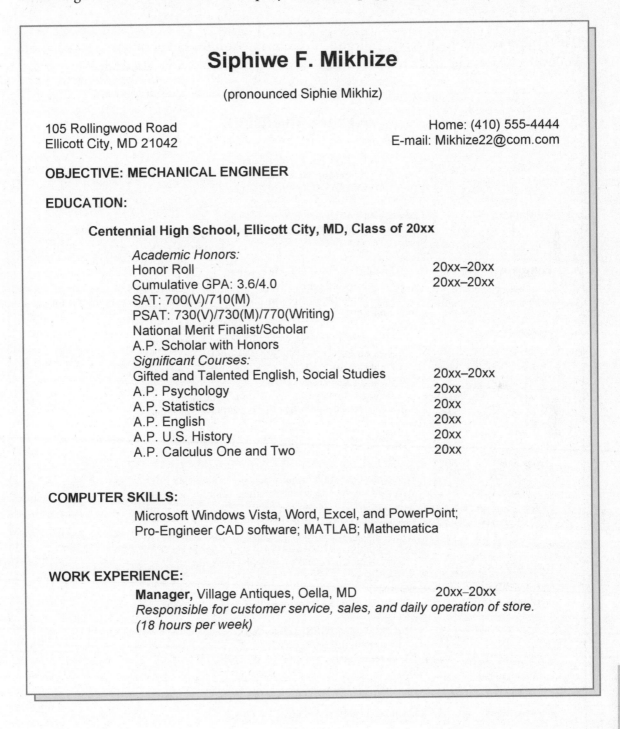

Siphiwe F. Mikhize

(pronounced Siphie Mikhiz)

105 Rollingwood Road
Ellicott City, MD 21042

Home: (410) 555-4444
E-mail: Mikhize22@com.com

OBJECTIVE: MECHANICAL ENGINEER

EDUCATION:

Centennial High School, Ellicott City, MD, Class of 20xx

Academic Honors:	
Honor Roll	20xx–20xx
Cumulative GPA: 3.6/4.0	20xx–20xx
SAT: 700(V)/710(M)	
PSAT: 730(V)/730(M)/770(Writing)	
National Merit Finalist/Scholar	
A.P. Scholar with Honors	
Significant Courses:	
Gifted and Talented English, Social Studies	20xx–20xx
A.P. Psychology	20xx
A.P. Statistics	20xx
A.P. English	20xx
A.P. U.S. History	20xx
A.P. Calculus One and Two	20xx

COMPUTER SKILLS:

Microsoft Windows Vista, Word, Excel, and PowerPoint;
Pro-Engineer CAD software; MATLAB; Mathematica

WORK EXPERIENCE:

Manager, Village Antiques, Oella, MD   20xx–20xx
Responsible for customer service, sales, and daily operation of store.
(18 hours per week)

College Fairs and Job Fairs

Admissions representatives and recruiters are waiting to meet you at these events. If you do not have a resume with you, you will not be very effective. This is your opportunity to introduce these individuals to your experience and interests.

At a job fair, your resume will be scanned into a database and kept for future job openings. At a college fair, the admissions representative will take your resume and use it to start a file on you in the college's office.

This type of resume is critical for college admissions, internships, and positions in corporations. Following is an example of a resume written for giving out at job and college fairs.

Kristen Bradshaw

1897 Rock Ridge Court
Glenelg, Maryland 55555
(555) 555-5555 kbrad@aol.com

Education	Glenelg County School, Glenelg, Maryland College Preparatory Program—Class of 20xx

Honors & Awards	Academic:
	    * First Scholar Award for two years
	    * French Award for two years
	    * High Honor Roll or Honor Roll and Effort Honor Roll every quarter for
	      four years
	Athletics:
	    * Varsity Field Hockey 20xx IAAM "B" Champions
	    * Basketball Coaches Award, 20xx/20xx
	    * Field Hockey MVP, 20xx
	    * Basketball MVP, 20xx/20xx
	    * JV Field Hockey Coaches Award, 20xx
	    * Varsity Basketball Most Improved Player, 20xx/20xx
	Arts:
	    * Music and Art Awards, 20xx

Experience October 20xx to January 20xx	* Triadelphia Ridge Elementary School, Ellicott City, MD World Cultures Mentoring Program—third-grade mentor

20xx to Present	* Wood family—(410) 333-3333
	    Babysitting 10-year-old daughter
	* Rogers family—(410) 444-4444
	    Babysitting 2-, 4-, and 6-year-old daughters

Extracurricular Activities	Leadership:
	    * Student Council & Business Partnership President
	Athletics:
	    * Field Hockey (GCS) Varsity & JV
	    * Basketball (GCS) Varsity
	    * Lacrosse (GCS) Varsity
	Other:
	    * Debating, Piano, Ballet, Psychology, and Travel

Certifications	Red Cross Basic First Aid and CPR (20xx)

Technical Training and Certification Training Resumes

Technical training programs consist both of class work and paid employment or an internship. These programs teach subjects such as automotive technology, computer graphics and design, accounting, and paralegal work. You might receive a certificate that can help you get a job in a specific technical field.

Filling out applications for technical training programs takes time. You can reference your resume to answer many questions and then attach a copy of your resume. Be sure your resume lists your related technical skills.

Take a look at the following sample resumes for some ideas of how a technical training resume might look and what to include.

John Mitchell
1 Main Street
Chesterfield, VA 23838
(804) 555-5555
mitchellj@aol.com

OBJECTIVE

To become certified as a daycare instructor and early learning educator, and eventually to obtain a B.S. in Early Education.

SKILLS AND COMPETENCIES

Patience and skill at working with young children.
Experienced with ensuring safety, discipline, and structure while giving creative learning opportunities.
Caring and nurturing attitude in classroom and play activities.
Able to follow curriculum and work to ensure learning goals are met through activities, small groups, and one-on-one.

EDUCATION

Matoaca High School, Chesterfield, VA
September 20xx–present

ACTIVITIES

DECA; volunteered for 20xx food drive for the homeless
Virginia High School Leadership Conference; Outdoor Track

EXPERIENCE

Goddard School, Chesterfield, VA
August 20xx–present; 20 hours per week
- Create and organize a planned schedule for the week to come
- Supervise a full classroom of 18 kindergarteners
- Interact and communicate with parents on a daily basis

GSI Commerce, Melbourne, FL
December 20xx–June 20xx
- Performed data input and analysis for catalog marketing company
- Provided top-notch customer service; effectively responded to customer concerns and questions
- Computer skills with Microsoft Excel and Microsoft Word; keyboard 50 wpm

REFERENCES

Available upon request

Tooraj Enayati

555 Pine Lane • San Antonio, TX 21228
Home: (555) 555-9999 • Work: (555) 555-2222
E-mail: enayati222@yahoo.com • U.S. Citizen

OBJECTIVE: A POSITION IN THE MUSIC INDUSTRY

TECHNICAL SKILLS

- Digital and acoustic music composition and arrangement
- Recording and engineering
- Sound system installation in homes and automobiles
- Internet and digital sound
- Excellent communications skills
- Creative and enthusiastic about quality and new projects and techniques

EDUCATION & TRAINING

Successfully passed GED, 20xx
Glendary Preparatory School, Howard, TX, 20xx–20xx
Manders Institute, Houston, TX, 20xx–20xx
Electronic and computer music workshops including Audio
Production, Sound Engineering, Composition, and Digital Music.
Private piano study (four years of music theory and piano
performance).

INTERNSHIP

Alpha School of Applied Recording Arts and Sciences,
San Antonio, TX, 12-week program, summer 20xx
Alpha is a major multi-studio complex with four professional
recording studios. Internship in recording and engineering under
acoustician James Garner. Assisted engineering for KHFS program
"Just Passing Through."

ELECTRONIC MUSIC EQUIPMENT

Home Studio with PC: Digital Sampler ASR 10, Denon 3-head,
2-track tape deck, NAD 1600 preamp, Nakamichi EQUIPMENTSTASIS
amp, Infinity Ref, Series II; PC with Cakewalk, Mackie 24x8, Alesis
Adat; Tascam DAT MK30II.
Performance: Keyboard, electric bass, various acoustic instruments.

AmeriCorps or National or State Community Service Resumes

As an AmeriCorps member, you will gain valuable experience in an area that interests you that can translate directly into job experience in your chosen field. You will learn teamwork, communication, responsibility, and other essential skills that will help you for the rest of your life while gaining the personal satisfaction of taking on a challenge and seeing results. Many find their AmeriCorps year provides them with more experience and skills than they would have gotten in a traditional paying job.

Do you want to serve your community or provide social or human services? Community services and volunteer work can give you qualifications, experience, and networks for your future career.

Consult the earlier volunteer and community services resume for some ideas of how to approach creating a resume for AmeriCorps.

Military Academy and Scholarship Resumes

It should come as no surprise that a resume might be useful when applying to a military academy or seeking a military officer scholarship to any number of select U.S. colleges or universities. The two main routes to becoming an officer right out of high school are going through the various service academies and receiving a college scholarship and involving yourself in an ROTC program at a participating college. All branches of the service have these avenues for you to consider. A resume will come in handy often as you are interviewed by the recruiters and perhaps congresspeople or their assistants in order to obtain a congressional nomination for an academy.

Each of your interviewers might choose to review your resume prior to your interview and hopefully use it as a primary reference point during the interview. It would be great to have each interviewer glance at the various subject categories listed on your resume and ask you questions about it. After all, you have put your resume together so that it best describes you in a nutshell, featuring the unique strengths that you possess.

In most cases, the interviewer wants to know your motivation for applying (which is covered in the objective), your academic standing and coursework strengths, and any other points that make you look particularly strong. The military services look favorably upon those who hold leadership roles, are involved in community and civic affairs, and have some athletic abilities.

To begin your application, check the various Web sites for each branch of the military. Each should have links for its application procedures and provide a timeframe for applying. For example, if you are interested in the Navy, the Web site is https://www.nrotc.navy.mil; the U.S. Naval Academy is www.usna.edu. Each branch has its own site for application; however, the actual application processes and necessary documentation required are very similar for all of them. The vast majority of your application will be completed online or attached to your initial file on the Web site.

The best time to apply to either the academies or their ROTC programs is during the spring of your junior year in high school. At that time, you should be at least 16 years old. If you are applying for the ROTC scholarship, you will simultaneously need to research the college admissions requirements for the schools where the scholarship is offered. The ROTC program leads to a commission as an active-duty officer in a branch of the military. You can take the scholarship only to a college affiliated with the program. You will have coursework requirements among other specific expectations you will need to maintain while on the scholarship.

The decision to accept or decline your application for a scholarship or appointment to the academy is 100 percent based on your application package as a whole. Only a fraction of your application package reflects your interview with the interviewing officers or congresspeople. That means your achievements as a high school student must be reflected fully and completely in the written word. The references required from your teachers, your application's statement of interest, test scores, grades, and so on are the factors used to represent you. So if you want to have a strong package for the selection board, you must show consistent effort and progress throughout all of your high school years, starting in ninth grade.

Understanding what types of high school classes and activities will best represent you, and are in turn most desired by the military services, will help you plan your courses each year through high school and also give you awareness of the areas you might need to put extra effort into. Look at a college course catalog online to see what you will be expected to take in your first year in high school. Make sure to do your homework and successfully complete all prerequisite courses you might be expected to have completed prior to beginning college work.

Additionally, the extracurricular activities you participate in will reflect a certain type of individual. The military services do not want athletes with low GPAs or out-of-shape academic achievers; they want well-rounded individuals. Try to represent a good balance of activities. However, be honest with yourself, and do not try to be what you are not. If you enjoy science and literature, for example, make the most of those interests. Join the science club and become an office holder. Participate in local, regional, and national science events. Go beyond the expected or the average and develop those specific interests in their broadest sense. It is better to show perseverance and commitment to your interests and causes than be scattered all over the page with too many activities and not enough true participation and achievement.

Following are sample resumes for applying to military academies and ROTC scholarships.

Mitchell S. O'Donnell

18739 Rose Hill Drive, Monticello, GA 30125
(888) 888-8888   mitch001@com.net

Objective

Acceptance as a candidate for the Class of 20xx U.S. Naval Academy or U.S. Naval ROTC scholarship program for year 20xx. To be offered the opportunity to receive an appointment to the Academy or selection to attend Naval ROTC would be a fulfillment of my personal discipline, hard work, and consistent efforts to achieve the highest standards possible.

Education

20xx–present   Gardendale High School   Monticello, GA
Expected Graduation: May 20xx   Present GPA: 3.56

Honors curriculum and Advanced Placement courses: Algebra II,
    Calculus, Physics, and Spanish II and III
National Merit Finalist/Scholar
SAT: 730 (V) 780 (M)

ATHLETICS:
* Varsity Football, 20xx–present
* Lifeguard at High School Pool, Summers, 20xx, 20xx
* Catcher on Little League Team, Summers, 20xx, 20xx
* Participated in 5K and 10K events throughout state, 20xx–present

Leadership Positions

* President, National Honor Society, 20xx–present
* Co-captain, Gardendale Varsity Football, Jr. and Sr. years
* Achieved rank of Eagle Scout, 20xx
* Established and chaired Environmental Action Team for city/county
* Representative at Boys State, Albany, GA, 20xx

NATHAN T. BROWN

Ramstein Air Base
APO AE 09094
(0049) 06371-1459475
brownn101@aol.com

OBJECTIVE: To join the U.S. Air Force as a military professional.

SKILLS SUMMARY

Analytical skills
Self-taught in some computer skills
Leadership and communications skills

Schematic readings and manuals
Strong technical and diagnostic skills
Keyboarding skills: 40 wpm

EDUCATION

Ramstein High School, Ramstein Air Base, Germany   Class of 20xx

Activities:
- JROTC Member; recognized for leadership and outstanding attendance award
- Junior Reserve Officer Training
- Member, Wrestling Team, 20xx to present
- Corps Drill Team

Area of Focus: Computer Technology Courses
- Computer Service and Repair
- Technology Learning Community
- CISCO Certification and Training
- Other coursework included building and troubleshooting computers; studying Windows; installing software

Honors & Awards:
- Merit Awards in Intro to Computer and Windows Vista Course

EMPLOYMENT

Computer Repair, Freelance, Ramstein Air Base and Vogelweh Housing Area, 20xx to present.
Troubleshoot, repair and assist with training in Windows, Word, and e-mail programs for friends. Hourly, $8.00

Electronics Set-Up Assistant, Ramstein Air Base, Civil Engineering, Summer 20xx.
Grounds maintenance, event set-up, electronic equipment set-up. Hourly: $8.00

ACTIVITIES

Summer Camp Counselor, The Ramstein Community Center, Ramstein Air Base, summer 20xx. Planned activities and crafts for children ages 6 to 12 in small groups.

LANGUAGES AND TRAVEL

Speak German moderately. Traveled throughout Europe for four years during summers and holidays. Experienced with cross-cultural environments. Enjoy military history and war-game scenarios and simulation systems. Member of the Ramstein Southside Fitness Center.

Government Jobs and Internships

The United States government is the largest employer in America, with 1.8 million employees. This does not include the U.S. Postal Service, the U.S. military, or contractors who work for the government. The government is hiring. You should consider government jobs or internships to begin your career and to gain valuable career experience and mentoring from industry experts. Government job searches are a little different than private-industry searches, but with effort, you can find an interesting and possibly good-paying position.

Jacques R. Revellier, IV
121 Robert E. Lee Hwy.
Bristol, VA 21117
(470) 555-8888
jacques4@com.com

OBJECTIVE: Biomedical Research Summer Internship

SUMMARY OF SKILLS

Laboratory:
- Prepared specimens for laboratory analysis and testing. Prepared and stained slides for microscopic testing for specific disease pathogens.
- Skilled in the use of laboratory equipment and instrumentation.
- Observe veterinary surgical procedures on both domestic and farm animals. Provide minor assistance as requested.

Animal Care:
- Caring attitude with pets and farm animals.

Computer:
- PC experience with Microsoft Word, PowerPoint, and Access.

Dependable, motivated, and eager to learn.

EDUCATION

High School Graduate, Williamsburg High School, Virginia—20xx
Courses: Biology, Biology Lab, Chemistry, Chemistry Lab, Zoology

EMPLOYMENT EXPERIENCE

NATIONAL HUMAN GENOME RESEARCH INSTITUTE, National Institutes of Health (NH), Bethesda, MD, 20xx Summer Internship Program; 8 weeks, 40 hours per week. This internship provided the opportunity to study and practice clinical research in human genetic disease. Received feedback from scientists on lab studies and test recording in biomedical research.

BOONSBORO ANIMAL HOSPITAL, Abingdon, VA; July 20xx to Present, 10 hours per week. Veterinary Assistant. Work directly with veterinarian to diagnose and treat a variety of domestic animal diseases and conditions. Assist with routine examinations and treatments. Maintain facility, lab, and equipment.

HO CLINIC, Ho, Ghana, West Africa; June 20xx to August 20xx, 40 hours per week. Three-month international volunteer assignment in a third-world African nation. Lived in African compound and worked at local veterinary hospital that cared for both animals and people because of their relatively modern laboratory facilities. Acquired outstanding hands-on experience in phlebotomy, hematology, routine and emergency surgical procedures, field autopsies, and general animal health care.

TRI-CITIES ANIMAL HOSPITAL, Bristol, Virginia; 20xx to 20xx, 10 hours per week. Animal Care Assistant. Worked weekends while in high school. Cared for domestic animals, cleaned kennel facilities, and provided routine hygiene. Pet intake and initial workup.

What's Next?

As you learned in this chapter, you can use a resume in many ways—not just for job searching. Start thinking about your resume now. The rest of this book gives you the how-to instructions for looking great on paper.

Chapter 2 will help you identify your best skills to include on your resume. Chapter 3 will help you understand two types of resumes you might want to use. Your resume will help you feel confident about your achievements, activities, skills, and interests.

Describing Your Skills

College admissions officers, internship coordinators, job recruiters, and managers review resumes for the best match between their opportunities and candidates' backgrounds. The skills that you offer such a manager/recruiter could help your resume stand out from the competition. Skills are important in a resume. That's why several chapters of this book cover skills:

- In chapter 1, many of the sample resumes include a summary of skills.
- Chapter 3 covers keywords, which many times are also skills.

In this chapter, I will talk about soft skills, hard skills, and competencies that can help your resume stand out from the competition for an internship, scholarship, job, or other opportunity.

Defining the Term *Skills*

Think of skills as being something you do well. In general, skills can be divided into two categories: soft skills and hard skills.

- **Soft skills:** These are skills that are part of your personality, such as being organized or being friendly. A barista must be a team player, be friendly, have a good memory, and be enthusiastic (and love coffee).
- **Hard skills:** These skills might also be called technical skills. Computer skills, science laboratory, research, writing, public speaking, and acting are examples of hard skills.

Soft Skills

You might not realize it, but you have many soft skills. Describing your soft skills is a good way to make yourself more appealing in the job market. Soft skills can be divided into two categories.

Adaptive Skills

Adaptive skills are also called personal skills. These skills are part of your personality. They help you adapt to different situations. Examples of adaptive skills include the following:

- Enthusiastic
- Energetic
- Friendly
- Outgoing
- Honest
- Dependable
- Physically strong and possessing stamina
- Able to learn quickly
- Sincere
- Patient and calm
- Empathetic (caring)
- Able to get along with coworkers
- Competitive
- Willing to work hard

Transferable Skills

Transferable skills are also called general skills. These are skills that can be used in many jobs. Examples of transferable skills include the following:

- Finishing assignments on time
- Working with people
- Flexibility
- Handling many projects at once (multitasking)
- Expressing yourself through art, music, dance, writing
- Staying organized
- Following instructions
- Paying attention to detail
- Speaking before groups
- Leading a club
- Writing clearly

Soft Skills Worksheet

Use the left column to list some of the soft skills you have. In the right column, give examples that demonstrate that you have these skills and have used them.

_____   _____

                            _____

                            _____

_____   _____

                            _____

                            _____

_____   _____

                            _____

                            _____

Hard Skills

Having specific hard (or technical) skills can help you get a corresponding job, so they are often referred to as job-related skills. Being extremely clear about your hard skills is important. A potential employer will appreciate seeing a list of these skills. Following are three examples of what a hard skills section of a resume might look like:

Skills Summary:
Leadership and organizational skills
Customer service and public relations skills
Computer skills: Microsoft Office; keyboard 50 wpm
Bilingual: Spanish and English

Summary of Skills and Experience:

Writing and Research
Skilled researcher in many of the basic subjects such as Biology, Chemistry, and different types of language arts. Three years of advanced English classes, which involved many research papers and language development skills.

Computer Skills
Completed two year-long courses in computer applications. These classes gave me knowledge and skill in Microsoft programs such as Word, Access, Excel, and PowerPoint. Experience with PC and Macintosh; Internet; superior typing skills.

Foreign Language Skills
Three years of high school Spanish.

SUMMARY OF SKILLS

- **Clerical:** File maintenance, office administration, mail management
- **Computers:** MS Office applications (including Word), keyboard 55 wpm, data entry, Internet
- **Organization:** Follow through on details, event planning, and coordination
- **Communications:** Telephone, customer service, team leadership
- **Personality:** Friendly, quick learner, dependable, hard worker

Hard Skills Worksheet

Use the left column to list some of the hard skills you possess. Target these to a specific field (pick something that appeals to you if you don't already have a field you intend to apply to). In the right column, give examples that demonstrate that you have these skills and have used them.

_____   _____

                                 _____

                                 _____

_____   _____

                                 _____

                                 _____

                                 _____

_____   _____

                                 _____

                                 _____

Important Work Core Competencies

The following work core competencies were developed for Veterans Health Administration affiliate hospitals. After it was found that the staff at VA hospitals were not being as caring, patient, kind, and efficient as they should have been, the hospitals' managers created a list of the most important competencies for all of their employees. Now all employees have to show that they have these competencies, or they will not get good performance ratings.

If you develop these work competencies, you will be a better employee and your supervisor's evaluations will be better. You can also write about these competencies in your resume. If you interview for a job, you can talk about these competencies and supervisors will be impressed. Interviewers like to hear that you are creative, are customer focused, and have excellent interpersonal skills.

The skills list here could be used by just about any employee for any position. Employers are looking for high-quality employees who can demonstrate these skills.

Technical Skills:

- Displays specific technical knowledge and skills to perform job duties.
- Understands processes and procedures.
- Keeps current on new products and processes.
- Effectively uses available technology (voice mail, automation, software, and so on).

Interpersonal Effectiveness:

- Builds positive relationships.
- Handles conflicts and negotiations effectively.
- Builds trust and respect.
- Collaborates and works well with others.
- Shows sensitivity and compassion for others.
- Communicates clearly—both orally and in writing.
- Listens actively to others.
- Honors commitments.

Customer Service:

- Understands that customer service is essential.
- Shows commitment to customer service.
- Listens to customer complaints and concerns effectively and promptly.

Flexibility/Adaptability:

- Responds appropriately to new or changing situations.
- Handles multiple inputs and tasks simultaneously.
- Accommodates new situations.
- Remains calm in high-pressure situations.
- Demonstrates resilience.

Creative Thinking:

- Demonstrates new ideas and approaches.
- Thinks and acts innovatively.

✎ Demonstrates willingness to take risks.

✎ Solves problems creatively.

✎ Demonstrates resourcefulness.

Work Core Competencies Worksheet

Pick out some of the work core competencies you possess and write them in the left column. Use the right column to detail how you have demonstrated these skills.

_____   _____

                       _____

                       _____

_____   _____

                       _____

_____   _____

                       _____

                       _____

What's Next?

In this chapter, you have learned to identify your skills. You studied several examples of how to list these skills on your resume. In chapter 3 you'll learn how to pick out keywords from job descriptions and use them on your resume. In chapter 4, you will see how to arrange the various sections of your resume. This is referred to as formatting. You will also find tips that will help make your resume attractive and readable.

Understanding Resume Types and Keywords

The sample resumes in chapter 1 can be divided into two formats:

- Targeted resumes
- Chronological resumes

The most popular resume format is the targeted resume with keywords. Most of the samples in chapter 1 used the targeted format with a Summary of Skills section. This is the type of resume that works best in most situations. A targeted resume includes a detailed summary of your skills using keywords from your selected industry. This skills summary is followed by information about your education and experience. This type of resume presents all relevant information in a way that appeals to the employer or individual you are targeting. The following situations require the targeted resume format:

- Job applications
- Internship applications
- Work-study and co-op applications
- Military scholarship applications
- National and community service applications

The second format is the chronological resume. This resume presents your education and experience without targeting a particular job, internship, or industry. Start with your high school information and end with your work history and volunteer activities. The following situations require the chronological resume format:

- College applications
- Scholarship applications

This chapter gives more information about creating targeted and chronological resumes.

Targeted Resumes

A targeted resume should be no more than one page. It highlights the skills and experiences you want to promote to a potential employer or mentor. You might not realize it, but you do have skills that can be highlighted! You have developed these special skills in many ways, including the following:

- School courses and projects
- Work experiences
- Internships
- Volunteer activities
- Extracurricular activities
- Interests and hobbies
- Sports
- Travel

Soft Skills, Hard Skills, and Competencies

Soft skills (also called competencies and personal traits) are personality-type skills—the skills that you have naturally. Examples are self-motivated, energetic, excellent communication, team-oriented, friendly, courteous, works well with others, flexibility, and sense of humor.

Hard skills are technical skills or skills that you learned on your own, through training, or in school. Examples are Microsoft Office, database applications, analytical skills, cash register use, writing, editing, public speaking, electronics, and welding skills.

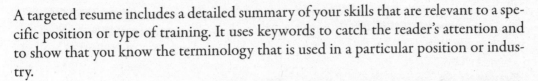

A targeted resume includes a detailed summary of your skills that are relevant to a specific position or type of training. It uses keywords to catch the reader's attention and to show that you know the terminology that is used in a particular position or industry.

You should list your most significant and special skills in a separate section. This skills section can help you stand out. Your skills are different from those of other applicants, and the recruiter might be looking for someone just like you! Most recruiters love having this information.

Example of a Skills Summary Section of a Resume with Keywords

Skills Summary

- Enthusiastic and energetic
- Excellent teamwork and interpersonal skills
- Organized and detail-oriented
- Excellent computer skills, including Word, Excel, and Internet research
- Customer service experience

Create your own list of some of your best traits. Try to think of how to word these as skills that could appeal to an employer.

_____   _____

_____   _____

_____   _____

_____   _____

Keywords

Keywords are the most pertinent words for a particular company or position. If you add certain keywords to your resume, you will get better results from your resume.

Keywords can be soft skills, hard skills, personality traits, and acronyms. They are the everyday words of the hiring manager in each situation. Add these words to your resume and you will stand out.

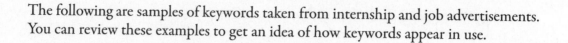
The following are samples of keywords taken from internship and job advertisements. You can review these examples to get an idea of how keywords appear in use.

Keywords for a Day Care Internship

SKILLS AND COMPETENCIES	**Patience** and skill at working with young children Experience with ensuring **safety, discipline,** and structure while giving **creative learning** opportunities **Caring** and **nurturing** attitude in classroom and **play activities** Able to **follow curriculum** and work to ensure **learning goals** are met through **activities, small groups,** and **one-on-one**

Keywords for Southwest Airlines Internship

Experience:
- Participation in **organizations** and **clubs** desirable
- Proficient with **Microsoft Office** applications
- **Database** applications helpful, but not required

Skills and Abilities:
- **Excellent communication** (reading and writing), **analytical,** and **organizational** skills
- Ability to **manage time** and **multiple tasks** effectively

Personal Traits:
- **Customer-service oriented**
- **Self-motivated and energetic**
- **Team oriented**
- **Ability to work equally well alone or with others**
- **Flexibility** to work in a dynamic, fast-paced environment
- **Sense of humor**

Job Duties:
- Projects include **research, presentation,** and **meeting** or involvement with or for **Engineering,** Hotels, **Safety, Training, Dispatch, Scheduling, ATC,** Navigation, or **Chief Pilots** (varies each term).

Keywords for Upscale Grocery Store Crew Member

Patriot Fred's is looking for part-time crew members in Virginia Beach, VA, to work in our grocery store! If you **like people, love food,** are **ambitious** and **adventuresome,** enjoy **smiling,** and have a strong sense of **values,** Patriot Fred's is definitely for you. Come be part of the excitement!

Our crew members participate in all aspects of store operations including **operating registers, customer service, product receiving, display building,** and **stocking**...but most important, our crew is responsible for making sure that our customers have a truly terrific shopping experience!

Who We're Looking For...The ideal crew member works with a sense of **urgency, loves food,** enjoys a **physically active** work environment, and has a **fun, positive personality.**

Keywords for Full-Time Cafe Hostess

Peacock Cafe is looking for a full-time hostess (min. five shifts per week) to **greet** our **patrons** with **energy** and a **smile.** We are looking for a **reliable** and **punctual** person who can relate to the **upbeat atmosphere** and **long hours.**

Keywords for Zoo Visitor Center Positions

Friends of the National Zoo, an exciting, dynamic, and diversified nonprofit organization located at the National Zoo, is holding a job fair to meet **energetic, friendly, courteous,** and **outgoing team players** for the following positions: Information Aides, Retail Sales Clerks, Food Service Associates, Parking Cashiers, and much more. **Punctuality** is required.

Keywords for Museum Gift Shop Worker

Busy museum gift shop now hiring salespeople to work year-round FT or PT in the Shops at Historic Mount Vernon, at the Home of George Washington.

Candidates must be able to **perform cash register transactions, provide good customer service,** and possess **outgoing, friendly personalities.**

Keywords for Tree Top Kids Sales Position

Tree Top Kids, a neighborhood toy store, is looking for **energetic** sales associates to join its **fun**-filled staff with a primary focus in the book department! Applicants must enjoy being around children, must be **attentive to detail,** possess **strong organization skills,** and be **comfortable using computers.** Responsibilities include **receiving deliveries and stock** in computer, **merchandising and shelving products,** and **communicating** with vendors regarding damaged/missing products. Applicants would also be trained to work on the sales floor, **assisting customers** and **ringing sales** through the register. Must be available mornings and afternoons. It's a great position to learn all aspects of the book business from checking in the new **inventory** to hands-on experience with the **customers!**

Keywords for Airport Team Members

Virgin America is a new travel brand that challenges industry norms in an attempt to deliver a more humane travel experience for the domestic traveler.

Main Purpose of the Role: Guest Services is a team of **energetic, focused,** and **flexible** people who have **fun** at what they do. Our role is to provide our guests with **personalized service** dedicated to ensuring that the entire travel experience is **enjoyable and hassle free.** The Airport Guest Services Team Member reports to the Station Supervisor, participates in a **"we" environment,** and is responsible for **customer service** at the airport. The Airport Guest Service Team Member must be an **assertive self starter** who **proactively** assumes responsibility for the airline's operational integrity and one who takes action to keep the airline safe, **on time,** and consistent with our values. The Team Member must be **highly organized, focused,** and **multitask** oriented with the ability to **prioritize tasks.** The position requires **quick thinking** and in-depth knowledge of **overall operations.**

Work and Life Skills Keywords for College Programs

Listed below are skill areas that some programs find useful and might seek in applicants. Please note that when you create an application, you will need to elaborate on each of the skills you have and give examples of when you demonstrated these skills.

- ❑ Architectural planning
- ❑ Business/ entrepreneur
- ❑ Communications
- ❑ Community organization
- ❑ Computers/ technology
- ❑ Conflict resolution
- ❑ Counseling
- ❑ Education
- ❑ Fine arts/crafts
- ❑ First aid
- ❑ Fund-raising/grant writing
- ❑ Law
- ❑ Leadership
- ❑ Medicine
- ❑ Public health
- ❑ Public speaking
- ❑ Recruitment
- ❑ Teaching/tutoring
- ❑ Trade/construction
- ❑ Writing/editing
- ❑ Youth development

Your Skills

Write down in the left column some of the skills from the preceding list that you feel you have. In the right column, add some explanation or examples of pertinent experience that illustrate that you have each skill.

Keyword Lists

Consider the following keywords for writing your resume and cover letter. And if you are invited to an interview, review the keywords to make sure you are ready to mention some of these words in the interview as well.

Keywords for Day Care Assistant

Patience

Safety

Discipline

Creative learning

Caring

Nurturing

Play activities

Follow curriculum

Learning goals

Activities

Small groups

One-on-one

Airline Internship

Organizations and clubs

Microsoft Office

Database

Excellent communication

Analytical skills

Organizational skills

Manage time

Manage multiple tasks effectively

Personal Traits:

Customer-service oriented

Self-motivated and energetic

Team oriented

Ability to work equally well alone or with others

Flexibility

Sense of humor

Job Duties:

Research

Presentation

Meeting

Engineering

Safety

Training

Dispatch

Scheduling

ATC

Chief Pilots

Keywords for Upscale Grocery Store Crew Member

Like people

Love food

Ambitious

Adventuresome

Smiling

Values

Operating registers

Customer service

Product receiving

Display building

Stocking

Urgency

Physically active

Fun

Positive personality

Keywords for Full-Time Cafe Hostess

Greet patrons

Energy

Smile

Reliable

Punctual

Upbeat atmosphere

Long hours

Keywords for National Zoo Visitor Center Positions

Energetic

Friendly

Courteous

Outgoing

Team players

Punctuality

Keywords for Retail Sales (Museum Gift Shop and Tree Top Kids)

Perform cash register transactions

Provide good customer service

Outgoing, friendly personality

Energetic

Fun

Attentive to detail

Strong organization skills

Comfortable using computers

Work Skills:

Receiving deliveries and stock in computer

Merchandising

Shelving products

Communicating

Assisting customers

Ringing sales

Inventory

Keywords for Airport Team Members

Energetic

Focused

Flexible

Fun

Personalized service

Enjoyable and hassle free

"We" environment

Customer service

Assertive

Self starter

Proactively

On time

Highly organized

Multitask

Prioritize tasks

Quick thinking

Overall operations

AmeriCorps Application

Teamwork

Communication

Responsibility

Taking on a challenge

Seeing results

Areas of Work Interest:

Architectural planning

Business/entrepreneur

Communications

Community organization

Computers/technology

Conflict resolution

Counseling

Education

Fine arts/crafts

First aid

Fund-raising/grants writing

Law

Leadership

Medicine

Public health

Public speaking

Recruitment

Teaching/tutoring

Trade/construction

Writing/editing

Youth development

How Do Your Experiences Relate to College Majors?

Think about what you would like to major in when you go to college. (If you don't have a major in mind, pick one that appeals to you for this exercise.) List below some of the experience, honors, or activities you have that might make you a more appealing candidate for this major.

_____

_____

_____

_____

_____

Summary of a Targeted Resume

Let's summarize. Keep these pointers in mind. A targeted resume

- Uses keywords relevant to the targeted position.
- Includes only those experiences that are relevant to the position.
- Should be only one page.
- Works well for people who are applying for jobs or for career training and in-service programs.

Emily's Targeted Resume

For the summer after graduation, Emily used the targeted resume on page 44 to apply for an internship at Kings Canyon, California. She wanted a position as a trail worker in the Volunteer-in-Parks Program, where she could gain environmental experience that involved hard labor.

This resume did not require specific information on honors, activities, workshops, and publications. Emily needed to show that she could backpack, navigate through rocks by making switchbacks, and live in a tent for two months.

Notice that the resume below uses keywords such as horse packing, minimum-impact camping, safety, and field hockey. These keywords reflect the skills needed for the trail worker internship that Emily wanted.

EMILY K. THOMPSON

43 Village Court
Westboro, MD 00000
Home: (000) 555-5555
ekthompson@gmail.com

OBJECTIVE: Trail Worker, Volunteer-in-Parks, Kings Canyon, California

SUMMARY OF RELEVANT SKILLS AND EXPERIENCE

Outdoor Leadership Experience
National Outdoor Leadership School, Lander, WY, (3 weeks training) Summer 20XX
Graduated Rocky Mountain Horsepacking course involving one week of ranch experience and two weeks of backcountry travel in the Wind River range. Trained in minimum-impact camping, backpacking, and horsepacking. Emphasis on backcountry leadership skills necessary to lead future personal expeditions: safety and judgment, leadership and teamwork, outdoor skills, environmental ethics, and horse handling and packing skills.

Interpretation Skills
Internship, Haleakala National Park, Maui, HI (12 weeks). Full-Time Work, Fall 20XX
Interpretation at high-volume visitor center and development of special projects, including park displays and 20-minute naturalist visitor programs. Hiked inside the volcano six miles.

High School Public Speaking
Experienced researcher and writer in high school and community publications. Four years of experience in theater and debate competitions.

Sports and Athletic Experience
Member, varsity field hockey team, 20XX. Enjoy hiking, backpacking, and camping. Physically fit.

EDUCATION

Westboro High School, Westboro, MD. Expect to graduate May 20xx.

WORKSHOPS

Hawaiian Language and Culture, Maui Community College, Maui, HI, Fall 20xx
Writing and Thinking, Lewis College, Seattle, WA, Summer 20xx
National Outdoor Leadership School, Lander, WY, Summer 20xx
Andre Brougher (*Homicide* series) Shakespeare Workshop, Winter 20xx
Writer's Workshop, State University, Frederick, MD, Summer 20xx

EXPERIENCE

Internship, Haleakala National Park, Maui, HI   Sept.–Dec. 20xx
Interpretation and special projects. Guide and Interpreter for 20-minute presentations daily.

Teacher's Aide, Newton Elementary School, Baltimore, MD   Spring 20xx

REFERENCES

Susan Wagner, Chief of Police, Haleakala National Park, Maui, HI, swagner@haleakala.gov

Chronological Resumes

A chronological resume is a comprehensive resume not targeted for a specific position, as it would be if you were pursuing a particular job or internship. It is a complete presentation of your achievements. It lists many items, including the following:

- Important academic courses and workshops
- Good grades
- Sports and other activities
- Honors and awards
- Work-study programs and internships
- Service learning
- Employment

This type of resume works well for people who are applying for college admission. You also can use a chronological resume to apply for scholarships, to find a mentor, or to distribute at college and job fairs. Your chronological resume, application, and personal statement will be your introduction to the people who make the admissions and scholarship decisions.

If you want to attend a particular college or training program, make your application package stand out. If you have a major or career interest in mind, make sure your resume includes all your experience, honors, and activities relevant to that major or interest.

Let's summarize. Keep these pointers in mind! A chronological resume

- Presents a broad, complete profile or review of your education, experience, activities, honors, and other background information.
- Is not targeted toward any particular job or career field.
- Includes a short summary of your skills.
- Can be used to apply for college or training programs, to apply for scholarships, to find a mentor, or to distribute at college and job fairs.

Emily's Chronological Resume

Emily used the chronological resume on page 46 to apply to colleges. Her interests in the environment have evolved. She hopes for a self-designed double major in environmental science and creative writing. In this resume, she moved the Education section to the top of the page. She emphasized her writing, teaching, and theater background because she planned to start her college career with the major in creative writing. Notice that she did not use the keywords she used in her targeted resume.

EMILY K. THOMPSON

43 Village Court
Westboro, MD 00000
Home: (000) 555-5555
ekthompson@gmail.com

EDUCATION

Westboro High School, Westboro, MD. Expect to graduate May 20xx.
Academic Honors:
Honor Roll, average GPA 3.8/4.0, 20xx–present
Advanced Placement: U.S. History and English coursework
Activities:
Editor-in-Chief, *Phoenix Literary Arts Magazine,* 20xx–20xx
Maryland State Forensics League, President
    Debate National Competitor: Kansas City, KS (20xx); Milwaukee, WI (20xx);
    Detroit, MI (20xx)
Dramatic Theater: *Twelve Angry Jurors; Flowers for Algernon;* and leading role in
    You Can't Take It with You

WORKSHOPS

Hawaiian Language and Culture, Maui Community College, Maui, HI, Fall 20xx

Writing and Thinking, Lewis College, Seattle, WA, Summer 20xx

National Outdoor Leadership School, Lander, WY, Summer 20xx

Andre Brougher (*Homicide* series) Shakespeare Workshop, Winter 20xx

Writer's Workshop, State University, Frederick, MD, Summer 20xx

HONORS AND RECOGNITION

Winner of Redmond College's "Women Writing about Women" Competition,
April 20xx, one of three selected out of 140 portfolios entered

PUBLISHED POETRY

Salt of the Earth literary magazine
Singing Sands Review
The Apprentice Writer
Featured reader in publicized Fells Point and Baltimore poetry readings

EXPERIENCE

Internship, Haleakala National Park, Maui, HI   Sept.–Dec. 20xx
    Interpretation and special projects. Guide and Interpreter for 20-minute presentations daily.

Teacher's Aide, Newton Elementary School, Baltimore, MD   Spring 20xx

REFERENCES

Karol Porter, English Chair, Westboro High School, (401) 333-3333, kporter@westborohs.edu

What's Next

You've seen several resume samples and studied the key features of targeted and chronological resumes. You can now integrate keywords into a skills section that will help your resume to stand out. It's time to start building your own resume—section by section—in the next chapter.

Writing Your Resume One Section at a Time

Building your resume one section at a time is the best way to remember all of the information you might want to add to it. Review the following sections and see whether you have added all of the important information you need to make your resume stand out.

Contact Information

A prospective employer needs to know how to contact you. The employer will want to see your name in large, bold type with your address, telephone number, and e-mail address clearly listed. Make sure your e-mail address isn't unprofessional (for example, avoid using an address like partygirl@aol.com). You can create separate e-mail accounts for college-, internship-, and work-related messages.

Following are three samples of contact information sections on resumes.

Kristen Bradshaw
1897 Rock Ridge Court
Marriottsville, Maryland 21104
Cell: (410) 555-7337
kb101@e-mail.com

CALVIN KLINE

2501B WHEATON WAY
DAVIS, CALIFORNIA 20000
(970) 555-0000
ckline101@yahoo.com

KYLIE MARIE JENNINGS

124 Hana Avenue, Haiku, HI • (555) 555-9999
E-mail: bigwave@net.net

Objective and Summary of Skills

If you are applying for a job, internship, co-op, or special program, you should include an Objective section on your resume. You will probably need to change the objective for each position that you apply to. Resumes should be focused toward each position.

You can also include a summary of your skills. You will need to change the summary of skills to add the keywords for the position or internship you are seeking.

Following are four examples of Objective/Skills sections.

OBJECTIVE:	To become certified as a daycare instructor and early learning educator; eventually to obtain a BS in Early Education.
SKILLS AND COMPETENCIES:	Patience and skill at working with young children
	Experienced with ensuring safety, discipline, and structure while giving creative learning opportunities
	Caring and nurturing attitude in classroom and play activities
	Able to follow curriculum and work to ensure learning goals are met through activities, small groups, and one-on-one interactions

OBJECTIVE

Internship program toward Certificate in Veterinary Training.

SUMMARY OF SKILLS

Laboratory:
- Prepared specimens for laboratory analysis and testing. Prepared and stained slides for microscopic testing for specific disease pathogens.
- Skilled in the use of laboratory equipment and instrumentation.
- Observed veterinary surgical procedures on both domestic and farm animals. Provided minor assistance as requested.

Animal Care:
- Caring for pets and farm animals.

Computer:
- PC experience with Microsoft Word, PowerPoint, and Access.

OBJECTIVE: A POSITION IN THE MUSIC INDUSTRY

TECHNICAL SKILLS
- Digital and acoustic music composition and arrangement
- Recording and engineering
- Sound system installation in homes and automobiles
- Internet and digital sound
- Excellent communications skills
- Creative and enthusiastic about quality, new projects, and techniques

---

ACADEMIC GOAL: To join AmeriCorps Vista for a one-year Community Service program. Enthusiastic, energetic, and willing to learn new skills for community service projects.

SUMMARY OF VOLUNTEER EXPERIENCE:

COMMUNITY SERVICE: Summer Of Service (SOS) in 20XX, I donated over 150 hours for community programs. Served as leader of church Youth Group 20XX–20XX and Praise Team leader 20XX–20XX (Christ Center Community Church). Active in food drives and other activities. Participated in projects at churches around Fort Collins involving service projects and fund-raisers (painting curbs, cleaning, and renovation).

FUND-RAISING: Throughout one project called the 24-Hour Famine, raised over $250 to benefit people in third-world countries. Received pledges from church members to abstain from eating for 24 hours to raise awareness and funds for starvation in third-world countries.

DISASTER SERVICES AND TEAM LEADER: Summer 20XX, Team leader for high school students. Cleaned burned houses for fire victims in Show Low, AZ, for one week. Participated in heavy manual labor, including clearing out burned rubble and trees from privately owned property. Assisted at Salvation Army in organizing and giving out clothing and food to fire victims.

TEAMWORK: Summer 20XX, attended missions trip to Juarez, Mexico, in order to assist an orphanage in its work and supply natives with eyeglasses. Participated in projects around the orphanage to clean and fix the property. Supplied eyeglasses at a local church to the Tarahumaran people.

Objective Statement Worksheet

Practice writing an Objective statement for a target goal. If you have a program or job you will be applying for soon, use that. If not, pick something that appeals to you. Look at the examples throughout this book to get some good ideas of what Objective statements should look like.

_____

_____

_____

Education

The Education section of your resume should include the name, city, and state of your high school and your expected graduation date. Also, list specific academic information such as college entrance test scores and special courses. You can list your GPA if it is over 3.0. Include courses in languages, advanced placement, computers, and electives.

Following are three sample Education sections.

EDUCATION:

Southmont High School, Tucson, AZ; Sophomore; expect to graduate June 20xx
College-preparatory classes; GPA 4.0 in arts curriculum; 3.8 overall

Education

20xx–Present   Gardendale High School   Monticello, GA
Expected graduation: June 20xx
Present GPA: 3.56

Honors curriculum and Advanced Placement courses: Algebra II, Calculus, Physics, and Spanish II and III.

National Merit Finalist/Scholar
SAT: 730 (V) 780 (M)

Education	Glenelg Country School, Glenelg, Maryland
	College Preparatory Program—Class of 20xx
Honors & Awards	Academic:

Academic:
* First Scholar Award for two years
* French Award for two years
* High Honor Roll or Honor Roll and Effort Honor Roll every quarter for four years

Athletics:
* Varsity Field Hockey 20xx IAAM "B" Champions
* Basketball Coaches Award, 20xx/20xx
* Field Hockey MVP, 20xx
* Basketball MVP, 20xx/20xx
* JV Field Hockey Coaches Award, 20xx
* Varsity Basketball Most Improved Player, 20xx/20xx

Arts:
* Music and Art Awards, 20xx

Education Worksheet

Use the following lines to list your educational experiences. If you already have a specific program or job in mind, list courses that are relevant to that goal.

_____   _____

_____   _____

_____   _____

_____   _____

_____   _____

_____   _____

_____   _____

_____   _____

Honors and Awards

Your honors and awards show that you have skills and are dedicated. List your honors and awards and include dates. For example, if you were a champion swimmer or received a certificate for participating in an essay contest, write that information in this section. You never know when you might need that item for a targeted resume. You can organize and edit the honors and awards list as needed when you write another resume for a certain purpose.

If you don't have honors and awards you can list now, think what you might do to earn this kind of recognition. Here are two examples of the honors and awards section of a high school resume.

HONORS AND AWARDS
Academic:
- First Scholar Award in 20xx/20xx and 20xx/20xx
- French Award
- High Honor Roll or Honor Roll and Effort Honor every quarter from 20xx–Present

Athletics:
- Varsity Field Hockey 20xx IAAM "B" Champions
- Basketball Coaches Award, 20xx/200xx
- Field Hockey MVP, 20xx/20xx
- Basketball MVP, 20xx/20xx
- JV Field Hockey Coaches Award, 20xx/20xx
- Varsity Basketball Most Improved Player, 20xx/20xx

Arts:
- Music and Art Awards, 20xx

ACADEMIC HONORS:

20xx–present   Gardendale High School   Monticello, GA
Expected Graduation: May 20xx Present GPA: 3.56

Honors curriculum and Advanced Placement courses: Algebra II, Calculus, Physics, and Spanish II and III.
National Merit Finalist/Scholar
SAT: 730 (V) 780 (M)

Honors and Awards Worksheet

Use the following lines to list your honors and awards. If you already have a specific program or job in mind, target the awards you list toward that goal.

_____   _____

_____   _____

_____   _____

_____   _____

_____   _____

_____   _____

_____   _____

_____   _____

Activities

By looking at your Activities section, employers and college admissions staff can learn what you like and what you can do. If you haven't been involved in student activities, consider joining a club or other group soon.

Following are some examples of Activities sections.

Activities

Sophomore Class Vice President—School Year 20xx–20xx
    Lead meetings, plan events, plan fund-raising.

Member of Future Business Leaders of America—School Year 20xx–20xx

Freshman Class Treasurer—School Year 20xx–20xx
    Handle budgets, fund-raising, and cash control.

ATHLETICS:

* Varsity football, 20xx–present

* Lifeguard at high school pool, 20xx–200xx

* Catcher on Little League team, 20xx–20xx

* Participated in 5K and 10K events throughout state, 20xx–present

Activities Worksheet

Use the lines below to list your activities. If you already have a specific program or job in mind, target the activities you list toward that goal.

_____   _____

_____   _____

_____   _____

_____   _____

_____   _____

_____   _____

_____   _____

_____   _____

Workshops and Lessons

If you are lucky enough to have completed summer programs and workshops, they look great on your resume. List workshops and lessons you have attended. Include the sponsoring organization or individual's name and the years you attended. Specialized training is offered in sports, computers, writing, languages, drafting, music, theater, and many other interest areas. If you haven't participated in workshops or taken lessons, think about taking advantage of opportunities available to you. Ask your teachers, counselors, coaches, and school sponsors about these opportunities.

Following are three sample summer programs and workshops sections.

WORKSHOPS

Smyth School of Art, Washington, DC, Summer 20xx—Studio Art and Photography
Costa Rica, South America, Summer 20xx—Spanish-Language Immersion

LESSONS: Private piano study (4 years of music theory and piano performance)

Outdoor Leadership Experience
National Outdoor Leadership School, Lander, WY, Summer 20xx
Graduated Rocky Mountain Horse packing course involving one week of ranch experience and two weeks of backcountry travel in the Wind River range. Trained in minimum-impact camping, backpacking, and horse packing. Emphasis on backcountry leadership skills necessary to lead future personal expeditions: safety and judgment, leadership and teamwork, outdoor skills, environmental ethics, and horse handling and packing skills.

Summer Programs and Workshops Worksheet

Use the following lines to list your summer programs and workshops. If you already have a specific program or job in mind, target the programs you list toward that goal.

_____   _____

_____   _____

_____   _____

_____   _____

_____   _____

_____   _____

_____   _____

Internships

An internship should be presented just like a job on your resume. Not every student will have intern experience. If you do, that's great! List your internship job title. List where you worked and when. Describe your areas of responsibility.

Following are two sample Internship sections.

Internship, Haleakala National Park, Maui, HI, Fall 20xx
Interpretation at high-volume visitor center with development of special projects, including park displays and 20-minute naturalist visitor programs. Hiked inside the volcano six miles.

INTERNSHIP

Alpha School of Applied Recording Arts and Sciences,
San Antonio, TX, 12-week program, summer 20xx
Alpha is a major multi-studio complex with four professional recording
studios. Internship in recording and engineering under acoustician James
Garner. Assisted engineering for KHFS program "Just Passing Through."

Internships Worksheet

Use the following lines to list any internships you have completed. If you already
have a specific program or job in mind, target what you list about your internships toward that goal.

_____

_____

_____

_____

_____

_____

Work-Study or Co-op Programs

A position held through a work-study program should be presented like a job on your
resume. Again, not every student will have this kind of experience. If you do, be sure
to include it in your resume.

Following are three sample Work-Study or Co-op sections.

Kaiserslautern High School
Work-Study Program. Serve as a troubleshooter, repairer, and user supporter at Kaiserslautern
High School student computer laboratories.

EXPERIENCE: Goddard School, Chesterfield, VA
                         August 20xx–present; 20 hours per week.
- Create and organize a planned schedule for the week to come.
- Supervise a full classroom of 18 kindergarteners.
- Interact and communicate with parents on a daily basis.

Electronics Set-Up Assistant	Ramstein Air Base, Civil Engineering, summer 20xx Grounds maintenance, event set-up, and electronic equipment set-up

Work-Study and Co-op Worksheet

Use the following lines to list any work-study or co-op programs you have completed. If you already have a specific program or job in mind, target what you list toward that goal.

_____

_____

_____

_____

_____

_____

Technical Training Programs

On your resume, describe any technical training programs in which you participated. List your technical training position. Include the company name, your job title, dates, and areas of responsibility. If you were in training most of the time, list the types of training you received. Include relevant courses, the company for which you worked, your title, dates, and areas of responsibility. If you were certified through the program (such as in CPR or cosmetology), be sure to list that information.

Following are two sample training program sections.

Manders Institute, Houston, TX, 20xx–20xx
Electronic and computer music workshops, including Audio Production, Sound Engineering, Composition, and Digital Music.

La Quinta High School, Davis, CA   *Class of 20xx; Good GPA*
Completed technical program focusing on Industrial Design and Automotive Diagnostics and Repair. Courses included Industrial Physics, Welding, Machining, Drafting, Automotive Drive Train/Heating/AC, and Diagnostics and Electrical. **GPA 4.0 in all technical courses.**

Technical Training Worksheet

Use the following lines to list any technical training programs you have completed. If you already have a specific program or job in mind, target what you list about the program toward that goal.

_____

_____

_____

_____

_____

_____

Volunteer and Community Service Work

Volunteer and community service positions are often the same as paid positions in terms of your duties within the organization. If you don't have this kind of experience, consider getting involved soon. Community organizations would be thrilled to hear from you, and it demonstrates that you are a caring, hardworking person.

Be sure to include all your volunteer and community service jobs on your resume. List the names of the companies or organizations where you did the work. For each position, list the dates and your title. Describe your duties. Add the description of your experience to your resume as you would for a paid job. This section of your resume might look like one of the following examples.

Community Service   * Coordinator of Atlanta Feed the Homeless Thanksgiving, 20xx–20xx
                      * Participated in humanitarian mission trips, Panama & Mexico, 20xx–20xx
                      * Musician with church orchestra (trumpet) for four years.

COMMUNITY ACTIVITIES

- Member of church youth group; active in food drives and other endeavors, including the following: Summer of Service (SOS), donated over 100 hours for community programs; participated in project personally raising $250 to benefit people in third-world countries.
- Cleaned burned houses for fire victims in Show Low, AZ, 20xx.

COMMUNITY SERVICE: Summer Of Service (SOS) in 20xx; I donated over 150 hours for community programs. Served as leader of church youth group for two years and Praise Team leader 20xx–20xx (Christ Center Community Church). Active in food drives and other activities. Participated in projects at churches around Fort Collins involving service projects and fund-raisers (painting curbs, cleaning, and renovation). Recognized for friendly, enthusiastic, and outgoing spirit to lead volunteers in fund-raising.

FUND-RAISING: Throughout one project called the 24-Hour Famine, raised over $250 to benefit people in third-world countries. Received pledges from church members to abstain from eating for 24 hours to raise awareness and funds for starvation in third-world countries.

DISASTER SERVICES AND TEAM LEADER: Summer 20xx, team leader for high school students. Cleaned burned houses for fire victims in Show Low, AZ, for one week. Participated in heavy manual labor, including clearing out burned rubble and trees from privately owned property. Assisted at Salvation Army in organizing and giving out clothing and food to fire victims.

TEAMWORK: Attended missions trip to Juarez, Mexico, in order to assist an orphanage in its work and supply natives with eyeglasses. Participated in projects around the orphanage to clean and fix the property. Supplied eyeglasses at a local church to the Tarahumaran people.

Volunteer and Community Service Worksheet

Use the following lines to list any volunteer or community service work you have performed. If you already have a specific program or job in mind, target which projects you list toward that goal.

_____

_____

_____

_____

_____

_____

Work Experience

The paid and unpaid jobs you have held while in school will be important for future employers, internship human resources staff, and college recruiters. They will look at the length of time you worked, including the number of hours per week. They will be interested in the skills you developed and used. And they will want to know whether you gained any new knowledge or skills in the positions. It is important to describe your duties and any accomplishments from your jobs.

Following are three sample Work Experience sections.

MAUI RETAIL CORP., Lahaina, Maui, 20xx to present
Retail Sales/Computer Assistant to the Regional Manager

- Provide friendly, enthusiastic, and responsive customer service.
- Perform computer research concerning inventory, costs, and store information.
- Research competitive companies, products, and catalogs via the Internet.
- Manipulate online data to create sales and financial reports.
- Develop formulas and create Excel spreadsheets, graphs, and reports for management and financial analysis by managers.
- Conduct retail sales, customer service, inventory control, and merchandising.

The Perfect Touch, Springfield, IL (15 hours/week)—July–October 20xx

Retail Sales and Cosmetics Consultant for Merle Norman Cosmetics.
Assisted with product merchandising, inventory control, displays, and customer service. Advised customers in product selection and assisted with make-up services. Excellent experience in a small shop with cosmetics. Recognized for professionalism, customer care, and flexibility when working for special events, including weddings and proms.

Work Experience   Chekmarc's Restaurant May 20xx–May 20xx   Palm Bay, FL
Busboy, Dishwasher
Cleared and cleaned tables. Greeted customers. Washed dishes. Dependable, fast, and followed sanitation rules.

Work Experience Worksheet

Use the following lines to list any work experience you have. If you already have a specific program or job in mind, target the job duties you list toward that goal.

_____

_____

_____

_____

_____

_____

Language, Travel, and Personal Interests

This information is extra added details that some students might not add to their resume. But if you can speak another language, that could be impressive for an employer or college. You can add your level of fluency. Travel experiences can demonstrate global knowledge and show that you have the ability to schedule and coordinate logistics of travel. If you are involved in a certain sport or interest, the employer might have the same hobbies. This could create a great conversation in an interview.

Following are three sample language, travel, and personal interests sections.

LANGUAGES AND TRAVEL:
Speak German moderately. Traveled throughout Europe for four years during summers and holidays. Experienced with cross-cultural environments. Enjoy military history and war-game scenarios and simulation systems. Member, The Ramstein Southside Fitness Center.

PERSONAL INTERESTS & GOALS:
I breed and raise purebred miniature dachshunds. I enjoy travel and experiencing other cultures and customs. I recently traveled to Latvia, my mother's ancestral home, and have traveled extensively throughout the United States. My future goal is to continue to help others through missionary work.

SKILLS

Languages: Fluent Spanish; currently studying Japanese
Computers: PCs with Windows, Excel, Word, Internet, and e-mail

INTERESTS

Extensive travel in the United States and South America
Hawaiian culture and history
Philosophy and environmental sciences
Outdoor activities, including hiking, camping, and biking

Language, Travel, and Personal Interests Worksheet

Use the following lines to list any languages you are familiar with, travel you have done, or personal interests that might be relevant to the specific program or job you have in mind.

_____

_____

_____

_____

_____

_____

Computer and Technical Skills

Computer skills are important for most positions. Even basic keyboarding skills of 40 words per minute (wpm) can be mandatory for many positions. An employer will be interested in the software you can use and your level of expertise. Technical skills can be mandatory for many positions. Create a clear list so that it is easy for employers to read.

Following are three sample technical skills sections.

Laboratory Skills:
- Prepared specimens for laboratory analysis and testing. Prepared and stained slides for microscopic testing for specific disease pathogens.
- Skilled in the use of laboratory equipment and instrumentation.
- Observed veterinary surgical procedures on both domestic and farm animals. Provided minor assistance as requested.

TECHNICAL SKILLS

- Digital and acoustic music composition and arrangement
- Recording and engineering
- Sound system installation in homes and automobiles
- Internet and digital sound
- Excellent communications skills
- Creative and enthusiastic about quality, new projects, and techniques

Computer Skills:
- Microsoft Word—keyboard 40 wpm and proficient with Word for research papers and projects
- Excel—experience in managing data and survey reports
- PowerPoint—basic training and experience
- Internet research, Web 2.0 communications

Computer and Technical Skills Worksheet

Use the following lines to list your computer and technical skills. If you already have a specific program or job in mind, target the skills you list toward that goal.

_____

_____

_____

_____

_____

_____

Putting It Together

Print your final draft and ask someone else to proofread it. Review the consistency of the format, punctuation, and editorial content. Make sure you have reviewed each of the sections in this chapter and included all of the information possible. Then proofread, proofread, and proofread again. Some employers will eliminate your resume if it has even one typo.

What's Next?

In this chapter, you have listed all the facts about your education, honors and awards, activities, workshops and lessons, internships, work-study or co-op programs, technical training programs, community service and volunteer experience, work experience, and technical skills.

In chapter 5, you will learn how to format all the information you have gathered for your resume.

Formatting Your Resume for Electronic and Paper Applications

In today's job search world, there are clearly two ways to write and submit a resume. The first is an electronic online resume for mega job sites such as CareerBuilder, Yahoo! HotJobs, and Monster. With these sites, you can set up a profile and submit your resume into a database. This type of resume is usually not formatted with special fonts, spacing, or indentations. You will see samples of the online resume format in this chapter.

The second way is the traditional paper resume. The paper resume is formatted and might include various kinds of fonts, bullets, and indentations. It should feature an excellent visual presentation. Resumes in this format can also be uploaded to some of the online job sites. You can also attach a Microsoft Word resume to an e-mail and keep the format and presentation. If there is the potential that the recipient doesn't have the Word program or the same fonts you used, you could convert your MS Word resume into a PDF file, which retains the formatting and fonts.

> **Tip**
>
> Most of the sample resumes in this book are in paper format. You can easily convert a paper format resume into an electronic format by copying and pasting the resume into a job site's resume text window and making a few adjustments. No special fonts are required for job sites.

Electronic Resumes

An electronic resume is a resume format that you copy and paste into an online resume builder or application. When preparing an electronic resume, be sure to emphasize the right keywords (see chapter 3 for more on this). Do not use formatting, indentations, or highlighting in the document.

Dos and Don'ts of Online Resumes

Dos:

- Use 12-point type.
- Use ALL CAPS for emphasizing headings, job titles, or other important information.
- Include keywords and skills that are of interest to the employer.
- After you copy and paste your paragraph into an online form, review for line breaks. Fix lines that are broken incorrectly.
- Be consistent in the number of returns between headings.
- Be consistent in using ALL CAPS headings and titles.
- Proofread carefully.
- Preview your resume to fix any formatting problems.

Don'ts:

- Don't use bold type.
- Don't indent or center any type.
- Don't use the automatic bullet feature in Word.

Sending Your Electronic Resume by E-mail

Be sure that a potential employer or university can receive and read your attached file. Review their instructions for e-mailing resumes before sending.

- Find out whether the company will accept a job application by e-mail. If not, you'll have to send your resume and letter in the mail (see "Paper Resumes" later in this chapter).

- Follow the organization's directions for submitting the resume.

- Find out whether the company accepts e-mails with attached files. Some companies will not open attached files at all.

- If you have saved your resume as a PDF file, ask whether the company will accept that format (many prefer .doc or .txt files).

- If an e-mail address is included in the advertisement, e-mail will be the fastest and often best way to submit your resume.

- In the subject line of the e-mail, state the job title and your name. For example, the subject line might be "Patient Services Rep—Susan Jones, Applicant."

Saving Your Electronic Resume

Here are some pointers for saving your resume so that you can easily modify and print it when needed.

- If you keep your resume on a hard drive, you should back it up on a CD and keep the backup somewhere safe.

- Keep a printed copy of your resume for reference.

- E-mail your resume to yourself or post it to an online storage site, so that it is available to you online anytime.

- Recruiters receive thousands of resumes that are titled resume.doc. This makes it difficult for them to find specific resumes in their database. Save your resume and other documents using your name, document title, and date, as in these examples:

> Jason_Smith_Cover Letter 02 02 09.doc
>
> Jason_Smith_References 01 21 09.doc
>
> Jason_Smith_Resume 02 01 09.doc
>
> Jason_Smith_Starbucks_Narrative 02 14 09.doc

Sample Electronic Resume

Following is a sample electronic resume for applying for admission to a four-year college after attending a community college.

```
CALVIN KLINE

2501B WHEATON WAY
DAVIS, CALIFORNIA 90210
(970) 555-0000
ckline101@com.com

CAREER GOAL

To enter an aeronautical program in college and gain
relevant work experience toward my goal of becoming a
commercial airline pilot.

TECHNICAL SKILLS SUMMARY

Automotive repair/restoration, drive train/heating/AC, and
diagnostics and electrical skills.
Skilled analyst and problem-solver.
Rebuild and restore custom automobiles, four-wheelers;
award-winner.
Computer skills: Microsoft Office, Excel, and Access

COMPETENCIES

Work well independently and as team member, self-motivated.
Welcome challenging projects.
Take responsibility and am detail-oriented.
Multitask, work hard, and manage time effectively.
Work well under pressure and am flexible in fast-paced
environments.

EDUCATION

La Quinta High School, Davis, CA: Class of 20xx
Completed Technical Program focusing on Industrial Design
and Automotive Diagnostics and Repair.

Courses included Industrial Physics, Welding, Machining,
Drafting, Automotive Drive Train/Heating/AC, and Diagnostics
and Electrical.
GPA 4.0 in all technical courses. Proven technical
capabilities.

HONORS & AWARDS

Merit Awards in Welding and Automotive.
Received three-year full scholarship to AIMS Community
College.
Won People's Choice Award in local 4 x 4 show for 1978 Chevy
Truck.
```

CERTIFICATE PROGRAM

Aeronautical Certificate Candidate
Accepted into Commercial Aeronautics Program, AIMS Community
College, Foresman, California. Beginning flight time.

EMPLOYMENT

Auto Technician
HIGHLINE MOTORS, Davis, CA—Summer 20xx
Install, repair, and maintain high-end import cars.

Craftsman
WOOD SHOP, Mead, CA—Summer 20xx
Crafted custom dashboards from quality hardwoods and
veneers.

Autotech Trainee
WILF'S EUROPEAN MOTORS, Mead, CA—Summer 20xx

SPORTS/SPECIAL INTERESTS

Purchase, repair, and sell custom-built automobiles.
Projects completed include a 1977 Porsche 930 and a 1976
FJ40 Four Wheeler—rebuilt and restored from the frame up.

Compete in local auto races.

Collect and ride dirt bikes.

High school sports included boxing and swim team.

Paper Resumes

A paper format resume is best for mailing or handing to a manager. You can also attach your paper-format resume to an e-mail as a Microsoft Word file. You can usually upload Word documents to online resume databases, too. The paper format resume is better looking, easier to read, and more impressive than the electronic resume.

Keeping a reader's attention focused on your resume is a challenge. The average length of time a person will spend reviewing your resume is 3 to 10 seconds. People are busy and have short attention spans. You will hold their attentions only if your resume is attractive, well-organized, and error-free. If your resume is disorganized or has any mistakes, the employer will probably just throw it away.

A good layout can enhance the content of your resume. An employer's eye will go to the top and center of the page, so your contact information should be in that position. Put other important details (such as your skills section) near the top of your resume to ensure that they will be read. Information at the bottom might be overlooked.

Two Basic Paper Resume Formats

Two basic resume formats exist for paper resumes. They are "traditional with bullets" and "left-column headings." Each resume format is easy to read and impressive.

You will find examples of these formats on the following pages. These resume formats are also included on the CD at the back of this workbook.

Traditional with Bullets

A traditional-with-bullets resume uses Times New Roman or another serif font that is easy to read. This format is best for resumes with a lot of text because the resume content covers most of the page. This resume has 1- or 1.25-inch margins on both sides.

Left-Column Headings

This easy-to-read format lists all of the major resume section headings in the left column. This format is good for resumes with less content. It helps fill the page when you don't have enough text. Also, the extra space makes the resume more readable.

Selecting Your Type Font

You can choose from a variety of fonts for your resume. Here are our recommendations on the two most common resume fonts.

Times New Roman

This font is very traditional and looks like book type. It is conservative and easy to read. Times has serifs, which means that the type has "stems" on its edges. Here is part of a resume in Times New Roman.

COMMUNITY ACTIVITIES
- Member of church youth group. Active in food drives and other endeavors, including the Summer of Service (SOS), for which I donated over 100 hours to community programs, and a project for which I personally raised $250 to benefit people in third-world countries.
- Cleaned burned houses for fire victims in Show Low, AZ, 20xx.

EMPLOYMENT
Administrative Assistant, 20xx to present (part-time)
Kemmer & Silver, Law Associates, Tucson, AZ; clerical and front-desk support.

Counseling Aide, Summers of 20xx and 20xx
Huntz Junior High School, Holton Hills, AZ; secretarial and general office support.

Arial

This font is more contemporary and is sans serif (without serifs), which means that the type has flat, even edges with no stems. It is very clean, bold, and rather assertive, as you see in the following example.

COMMUNITY ACTIVITIES
- Member of church youth group. Active in food drives and other endeavors, including the Summer of Service (SOS), for which I donated over 100 hours to community programs, and a project for which I personally raised $250 to benefit people in third-world countries.
- Cleaned burned houses for fire victims in Show Low, AZ, 20xx.

EMPLOYMENT
Administrative Assistant, 20xx to present (part-time)
Kemmer & Silver, Law Associates, Tucson, AZ; clerical and front-desk support.

Counseling Aide, Summers of 20xx and 20xx
Huntz Junior High School, Holton Hills, AZ; secretarial and general office support.

Type Style

Bold, *italic,* ***bold italic,*** ALL CAPS, and SMALL CAPS are type styles that you can use to emphasize certain text on your resume. Be consistent with the use of type style. For example, if you use bold and all caps for one job title, use bold and all caps for every job title. If you use italic for your position titles, do so each time.

Bold

You can use bold type to highlight major headings, school and employer names, titles of positions, and any other information you want to stand out. For example:

Glenelg Country School, Glenelg, MD

Italic

Latin words such as *magna cum laude* and the names of fraternities or sororities are usually printed in italic. Italic type is harder to read, so use it sparingly. Here's an example:

Graduated *summa cum laude,* 20XX

Bold Italic

Bold italic is useful for secondary headings. A typical use for bold italic is the titles of positions:

Hostess, Edison Assisted Living Center

All Caps

When the type style is "all caps," the size of each letter is the same. Major headings are usually in all caps. Sometimes previous employers' names and the name of your school can be in all caps. Examples:

EDUCATION

COMMUNITY SERVICE

COMPUTER SKILLS

Small Caps

When the typestyle is "small caps," all of the word or phrase is in capital letters. However, the first letter of each word is slightly taller than the other letters in the word. Using small caps is another way to emphasize titles, names, and section headings. Examples:

SUSAN M. GOWER

EDUCATION

WORK EXPERIENCE

Point Size

Point size refers to the size of the letters. Typically, 12-point type is used for resumes; 11-point type is acceptable if you need to fit a great deal of information on one page. You might want to set your name in 14-point type so that it stands out. The headings for your resume could be in 12-point type with the rest of the resume in 11-point type for extra emphasis on the headings.

This chapter contains formatting guidelines, not formatting rules. Use your creativity to adapt these guidelines to your situation.

Layout

Layout is the overall design of the resume. It includes the placement and alignment of various elements of your resume. Be consistent with your layout. For example, use the same amount of spacing between each section of your resume.

White Space

White space between and around sections of your resume makes your resume easier to read. Between resume sections, allow a return. Spacing between employer names and job titles can also be a return if space permits.

Too much white space causes a resume to look skimpy. Too little space makes it look busy and cluttered. Use your judgment to obtain an easy-to-read mix of words and white space.

Margins

The usual margins are 1 to 1.25 inches at the top and bottom and on both sides. You can adjust these according to how much text you have.

Paragraphs

Paragraphs can be written in block style or with bullets to highlight every sentence, as you see in the following samples.

WORK EXPERIENCE

ACTIVITIES ASSISTANT, Goddard School, Chesterfield, VA, August 20xx–present; 20 hours per week

- SCHEDULING: Create and organize a planned schedule for the week to come. Coordinate with other teachers and specialists to organize student schedule for daily activities.
- CHILDCARE SUPERVISION: Supervise a full classroom of 18 kindergarteners. Interact and communicate with parents on a daily basis.

ADMINISTRATIVE ASSISTANT, GSI Commerce, Melbourne, FL, December 20xx–June 20xx

- DATA ENTRY: Performed data input and analysis for catalog marketing company.
- CUSTOMER SERVICE: Provided top-notch customer service; effectively responded to customer concerns and questions.

EMPLOYMENT

MAUI RETAIL CORP., Lahaina, Maui, 20xx–present

RETAIL SALES / COMPUTER ASSISTANT to the Regional Manager

COMPUTER RESEARCH: Research inventory, costs, and store information. Research competitive companies, products, and catalogs via the Internet.
SALES REPORTS: Manipulate online data to create sales and financial reports. Develop formulas and create Excel spreadsheets, graphs, and reports for management and financial analysis by managers.
SALES AND CUSTOMER SERVICE: Conducted retail sales, friendly customer service, inventory control, and merchandising.

Employment

The Perfect Touch, Springfield, IL (15 hours/week)—July 20xx–October 20xx

RETAIL SALES AND COSMETICS CONSULTANT, Retail Sales, Merle Norman Cosmetics.
PRODUCT MERCHANDISING. Assisted with product merchandising, inventory control, displays, customer service, and retail sales.
COSMETICS CONSULTING. Advised customers in product selection and colors, and assisted with makeup services.
SPECIAL EVENTS. Recognized for professionalism, customer care, and flexibility when working for special events, including weddings and proms.

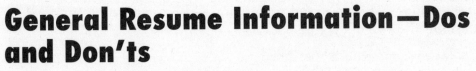

General Resume Information—Dos and Don'ts

Following are some general guidelines regarding resume content.

Resume Content Don'ts

Keep these resume don'ts in mind:

- Don't include your birth date or a photograph of yourself. Equal Employment Opportunity laws state that employers cannot discriminate against people because of their demographics. Including information about your age or a picture that shows your race places the employer in an awkward position.

- Don't include statements about your health, unless you're applying for a physical job.

- Don't include your Social Security number. Give it to an employer on your application if requested. If you apply for a federal government internship, you will have to add your Social Security number on the application.

- Avoid writing anything negative. You don't have to tell the employer everything, so don't include less-than flattering information, such as negative reasons for leaving a job or a low grade-point average.

Resume Content Dos

- State your objective carefully. An objective is optional but helpful. Your objective should state the type of position you desire.

- Keep the resume to one page if possible.

- Be sure your resume is error-free. Refer to the dictionary and your grammar books as needed. Run your software's spell checker.

- Beware of spell checkers. They won't catch errors in which you have used the wrong word, such as "there" instead of "their."

- To check each word's spelling, start at the bottom and read your sentences backwards. You will pick up words that don't make sense. This helps you focus on each word and not be distracted by the context.

- Have a friend, teacher, or parent read your resume to make sure the grammar, the punctuation, and all details are correct and consistent. This is extremely important! You can easily miss errors in simple things such as your phone number and employment dates.

- Use good white or off-white cotton bond paper.

- If you mail your resume, include your return address on the cover letter and on the top-left corner of the envelope.

- On the envelope, write a brief description of what is enclosed. For example, you might write "Enclosed: Application for Cashier Position."

- Always be honest.

Tip Update your resume at least once a year. Add new courses, workshops, community service positions, honors, activities, and jobs.

Writing Lessons

This section covers common errors in grammar and punctuation. If you don't have strong skills in reading and writing, have someone else read your resume to be sure it is correct and consistent.

Personal Pronouns

You do not have to use the personal pronoun "I" to begin statements in a resume. For example, here's the incorrect way to write the duties of a customer service position:

- I received inbound telephone calls and answered customers' questions.
- I searched the computer system and gave account information.
- I followed up and mailed corrected statements.

The following sound much better. The emphasis is on your performance and skills:

- Received inbound telephone calls and answered customers' questions.
- Searched the computer system and gave account information.
- Followed up and mailed corrected statements.

Verbs

For the job you have now, start your sentences with present-tense verbs. For jobs you had in the past, start your sentences with past-tense verbs.

The following Work Experience section includes two positions. One position is current and the verbs are present tense. The second position is past and the verbs are past tense.

EXPERIENCE	Goddard School, Chesterfield, VA
	August 20xx–present; 20 hours per week
	- Create and organize a planned schedule for the week to come
	- Supervise a full classroom of 18 kindergarteners
	- Interact and communicate with parents on a daily basis
	GSI Commerce, Melbourne, FL
	December 20xx–June 20xx
	- Performed data input and analysis for catalog marketing company
	- Provided top-notch customer service; effectively responded to customer concerns and questions
	- Computer skills with Microsoft Excel and Microsoft Word; keyboard 50 wpm

Colons

Do not use a colon after resume headings. This makes the resume cleaner with less punctuation.

Ampersands

An ampersand takes the place of the word *and*. Ampersands are not appropriate in the body text of a resume. However, you can use them to save space in headings, such as the following:

Writing & Editing

Travel, Languages & Interests

Honors & Activities

Word Confusion

Some errors can be found only by reading the words in the resume in context. The spell checker often doesn't pick up the differences in words that sound the same. Consult a grammar book or dictionary as needed. Here are some words that are commonly confused.

Contraction	Possessive
they're	their
it's	its
you're	your
who's	whose

Putting It Together—Resume Checklist

Now it's time to put together your resume. From the preceding chapters, we have worked on the following major items for your resume:

Producing and Writing Your Resume Content

Contact Information

Objective and Summary of Skills

Education

Honors and Awards

Activities

Workshops and Lessons

Internships

Work-Study or Co-op Programs

Technical Training Programs

Volunteer and Community Service Work

Work Experience

Language, Travel, and Personal Interests

Computer and Technical Skills

Reviewing for Format, Grammar, and Keywords

Research and add keywords to your resume

Check grammar, consistency, and punctuation

Check format online for consistency

Check spacing for consistency

Spell-check

Proofread and edit

 The samples in this book are on the CD-ROM. Open up one of the samples on the CD-ROM and replace the text in the resume to build your own resume draft. This is a fast way to start your resume.

Follow one of the samples from this book and type all of your resume information. Be sure to proofread and have someone else proofread your resume. Your future employer, internship manager, or college admissions officer will not be impressed with any typos, grammatical errors, or inconsistencies in format.

What's Next?

By the end of this chapter, you should have the basic information and format for your resume. It might be your first one. In chapter 6 you'll see several examples of complete resumes and the stories behind them. In chapter 7, you will learn to prepare cover letters, reference lists, and thank-you letters. These are tools you will use with your resume.

High School and College Student Resume Case Studies

In this chapter, you will see several high school and college student resumes. These resumes reflect the situations and abilities of actual students (the names and faces have been changed). Some of the students have accomplished a lot during their high school and college years. You will be impressed with the dramatic increase in the students' work-related activities during college. Students typically become more and more involved in activities, jobs, and programs, as reflected by the resumes.

The resumes in this chapter will probably not match your situation or plans exactly. But they will give you some ideas about what you can do, and how you might organize your resume. With a good resume, you can look for internships, quality community service assignments, or jobs. You can distribute your resume at job or college fairs and keep track of your high school accomplishments with it.

Lynda Teals, age 18, high school senior

Pursuing a College Degree in Fashion Design and Related Jobs

Lynda Teals has been acting since she was five years old and modeling since she was 13. Being on stage is Linda's passion. She has continued to act and model, and she also gained some professional training. She will be pursuing freelance or full-time modeling and acting opportunities while she goes to college. Living abroad with her military parents gave her some unique opportunities to model for foreign catalogues and magazines at a young age.

Currently, Lynda works at a clothing store at a local mall, where she excels in fashion. She enjoys helping others select and feel good in fashionable clothes. When she sends her resume to a modeling agency, it accompanies a full pictorial portfolio of her in varied attire, sample pictures of her runway modeling experiences, some selections from previously printed magazines and catalogues, and letters of reference. Her resume is formatted for modeling agents.

She enjoys design, fashion, and modeling and will apply to colleges to pursue a degree in fashion design or drama/theater (she is also considering becoming a drama teacher) to pursue her passion for the industry. Her well-rounded modeling, theatrical, and customer service experience will be an asset to her future aspirations.

LYNDA S. TEALS

1286 TYLER ROAD
ANAHEIM, CA 92807

555.555.5555
LYNDASTEALS@YAHOO.COM

Resume for Runway or Magazine Modeling
Attn: John Robert
555 Litton Way, Ste. 290, Anaheim, CA 92122
Studio: 555-555-5555

Education (09/20xx–06/20xx)
Canyon High School, Anaheim, California
Department of Defense High School (Japan & Germany)
- Honor Roll | Dean's List | Women's Volleyball

Experience (02/20xx–present)
Limited Too, Brea Mall, California
Customer Service Representative
- Assist customers with clothing selections. Operate a cash register and process credit cards and make change.
- Receive inventory, sort and count inventory, and place inventory in the store. Develop appealing displays.

Training
* Runway	Jim Crawford JR PLA JOLLA
* Acting	Darmstadt, Germany, Middle School Acting Class
* Voice	Coach Rachel Ketterlinus—Darmstadt, Germany
* Dance	Coach Trisha Crockett—Eastlake High School, California

Modeling
* Angelet Catalog
* *Sesame Magazine*
* Sugar and Spice Modeling Agency—Tokyo, Japan
* The Big Dream Bill Board & Flyers

Theatre
* Shakespeare Who?	Roles: Juliet—lead Lady Macbeth—lead	Darmstadt Performing Arts Center/ Elle Shepard
* Jack and the Beanstalk	Role: Merchant	Missoula Children's Theatre/MCT
* Cinderella	Role: Evil Stepsister	Rachel Ketterlinus/DMS
* Winter Arts Festival	Role: Chorus Member	Lynn Bales/DMS
* Back to the Fifties	Role: Fifties Girl	Hal Leonard Corporation

Special Skills
* Volleyball, Singing, Jazz Dancing and Ballet, Beginner Piano and Flute

Particulars
* Height: 5'11" | Weight: 125 | Hair Color: Black | Eye Color: Brown

Resume designed and edited by Diane Burns

Hannah Mellon, age 18,
high school senior

Pursuing a College Degree in Writing, Art, or Psychology

Hannah Mellon has been writing poetry, short stories, journals, and character sketches for many years. She is passionate about writing and she has won a number of writing awards. She will be pursuing her interest in writing while she goes to college. Hannah also plays the drums and has an avid interest in alternative music; she hopes to continue her pursuit of music, as well as her interest in psychology, and hopes to combine these interests with her interest in writing.

Currently, Hannah is on the editorial board of her school literary magazine; she is also on the executive board of Writers' Showcase, a group that selects individual creative-writing pieces to be acted on stage. She also enjoys helping others and is involved with several community art therapy programs. Hannah has been engaged in Hurricane Katrina recovery efforts. She has traveled to the Gulf Coast twice and has lent much-needed support and assistance to groups such as Habitat for Humanity and Volunteers of America.

404 Green Street
Evans, Illinois 80701
Phone 801-123-4567
Mellonh11@yahoo.com

Hannah Mellon

Education	20xx–present Evans High School, Evans, IL Diploma expected 6/20xx Honor roll; numerous honors classes
Awards received	20xx • 1st place writing award from English Department for character sketch • STATE Awards for academics and merit 20xx • Awards in chemistry and metal sculpture • Sophomore Honor Society • STATE Awards for academics and merit 20xx • Honorable Mention, Chicago History Fair • Nominated, Volunteer of the Year • STATE Awards for academics and merit
Interests and activities	Different creative activities such as playing musical instruments, drawing, and making short films.
Languages	Spanish (intermediate)
Volunteer experience	Traveled to Gulf Coast twice to participate in Hurricane Katrina relief efforts. Assist with creative arts expression and art therapy programs for youth.
References	William Bolsen: 801-846-8896 William Farmer: 801-424-7117 x4444 Nancy Wojcik: 801-824-6772
Extracurricular activities	Editor, Evans High School Literary Magazine, *The Paper Clip* Writers' Showcase Executive Board AYSO soccer

Resume designed and edited by Nancy Segal

Marcus Zyons, age 18, high school senior

Pursuing a Degree in Communications/ Broadcast Journalism

Marcus Zyons had a very specific goal: to become a broadcast journalist. He targeted one university and completed the appropriate applications. He was accepted and received a full scholarship. He pursued many opportunities during his middle school and high school years to engage in journalism learning opportunities (print and broadcast), which most likely helped his applications for scholarships.

His resume is full of educational highlights specific to journalism, including his honors and myriad activities. He also listed both paid and volunteer work, as well as his European travels.

Currently at his high school, Marcus is on the newspaper staff as a writer and serves at the campus radio station as a broadcaster. He also has a special pass to be on the football field and in the gym at all sporting events on the campus, and at the community football field. "When I graduate, I'll pursue bachelor and master degrees and move to New York City for a job in broadcast journalism," Marcus said.

MARCUS F. ZYONS

2876 Thunder Hill Road
Columbia, MD 20145

555.555.5555
marcus@yahoo.com

OBJECTIVE

ADMISSION TO UNIVERSITY OF MARYLAND UNDERGRADUATE PROGRAM

Major: Communications
Specialty: Broadcast Journalism

EDUCATION

Including Activities, Honors, and Distinctions

West County High School, Connelly Springs, MD   09/20xx to 06/20xx

12th Grade, Planned Activities (Will complete 12th grade in 20xx)
- Newspaper Sports Editor (selected for 20xx/20xx school year)
- Key Club (selected as member for 20xx/20xx school year)

11th Grade Accomplishments (Current GPA: 3.75/4.0)
- Who's Who Among American High School Students Honor Society (20xx)
- National Honor Roll
- Newspaper Sports Editor (Authored 13 articles)
- Key Club

10th Grade Accomplishments
- Who's Who Among American High School Students, 20xx
- National Society of High School Scholars, inducted in 20xx as a lifetime member
- National Honor Roll
- Newspaper Reporter (Selected one year early; newspaper positions are reserved for 11th and 12th graders)
- Key Club

9th Grade Accomplishments
- Men's Varsity Basketball Statistician
- National Honor Roll

ON ASSIGNMENT WITH NICKELODEON

Nickelodeon Studios, VIACOM Building, New York City, New York   06/20xx to 09/20xx
- Selected as one of seven of the first team of Nickelodeon GAScasters (game and sportscasters) in the nation, after an audition. Sent to New York City for training by broadcast professionals including CBS Sports Reporters, at the Nickelodeon studios.

Marcus F. Zyons, Page 2

- Attended a press conference with NY Giants NFL Cornerback (defensive back), and NY Liberty Point Guard. Vied for responses from other sports celebrities at the press conference, competing with members of the press from the *New York Times*.
- Interviewed Teresa Weatherspoon in a one-on-one 15-minute interview.
- Interviewed National Motocross Champion as a GAScaster interviewing a local athlete. The interview is the model interview format (train-the-trainer video) for all GAScasters to date (interview aired in October 20xx and in 20xx).
- Charter Communications used a clip of the Weatherspoon interview in a commercial for the Charter Cable TV channel (20xx).

ARTICLES

- *The News Herald,* **"Superstar Turns Out to Be Just Like Everyone Else" (20xx)**
  Interviewed Carolina Panthers NFL star Mike Minter.

- *Nickelodeon Magazine: Special Edition, Rocket Power,* **"Look at the Gold Medalist" (20xx)**
  On assignment as a GAScaster (kid's sports reporter) from Nickelodeon GAS: Games and Sports for Kids. Interviewed BMX Gold-Medalist, at the request of the editor of *Nickelodeon Magazine.*

PUBLICITY

The News Herald – About West County, "Child's Play Turns to Real Deal" (20xx)
Feature story about me while interviewing host of Nickelodeon's GAScasters, during training
in New York City

COMMITMENT TO THE COMMUNITY

West County Public Library, Volunteer, Summer 20xx Reading Program

EUROPEAN TRAVEL

Traveled to Germany, Italy, and the Czech Republic in May 20xx. Visited various European cities
including Rothenburg, Colmberg, Kitzingen, Wurzburg, Venice, and Prague. Stayed in a German
farm village for two weeks, met German locals, and enjoyed the culture.

Resume designed and edited by Diane Burns

David Myers, age 18, high school senior

Pursuing a Job in Music Before Starting College

David lived overseas for many years and attended a U.S. military school in Germany. David is an avid jazz musician and travels to jazz festivals throughout the United States. He was recently scouted to attend a private music school on scholarship and serve as the school's sole guitarist. David has also received individual training from a lead guitarist in a well-known platinum-selling band.

In high school, David's work experience has been limited to laborer, electrician intern, and custodian. But he did develop customer service and hard working skills in part-time summer jobs that he would now like to use in a sales associate position in a musical instrument store to help save money for college. He is also organizing a sideline tutoring class for beginning guitar players.

David already took his SAT and will start applying to music colleges around the country to pursue a career in music theory and composition, and a credential in teaching, so that he can become a music teacher in a middle or high school or junior college. He will continue to play at local events, including weddings and other parties, as a jazz musician or as part of local bands.

DAVID MYERS

5560 S. Lucky Avenue
Columbia, MD 21045
410.555.5555
davidmyers@comcast.net

OBJECTIVE & SKILLS OVERVIEW

Entry-level, part-time position in a music store or as a beginner guitar tutor.
Hard worker; very detail-oriented, polite, and respectful.
Willing to learn new skills. Culturally adept.

EDUCATION

Arts East Music School, Columbia, MD (Private music school)	06/20xx to 06/20xx
Centennial High School, Columbia, MD	09/20xx to 06/20xx
Department of Defense Dependent Schools, Wurzburg, Germany	10/20xx to 07/20xx

❏ Jazz Choir & Band (play the guitar for the Jazz Choir / Tour & play at Jazz Festivals in the USA)
❏ Play the guitar at local "gigs" (The Big Easy [Kid-Aid fund-raiser], local state fair, weekly Jazz
　　Night at the Coffee House, and weddings/parties)
❏ 4 years of German

EXPERIENCE

Laborer　　　　　　　　　　　　　　　　　　Summer 20xx/7 weeks
Jones Trucking, Baltimore, MD
Reference: Doug Lambert. Phone: 410.555.5555
Hours per week: 40. Salary: $300 per week
  ▪ Unloaded frozen food boxes from up to 4 semi-tractor trailer trucks into freezers daily.
  ▪ Labeled boxes with stickers and stamping equipment; labeled individual food containers.
  ▪ Counted and recorded the net weight of items removed from trucks; stacked boxes on
　　　pallets, and wrapped pallets in plastic wrap.

Internship/Electrician　　　　　　　　　Summer 20xx / 6-week program
Department of Public Works, U.S. Army Europe, Wurzburg, Germany
Reference: Jim Burts. Phone: 210.555.5555
Hours per week: 40. Salary: $5 per hour
  ▪ Worked side-by-side with experienced electricians and learned about basic electrical
　　　circuitry. Installed ceiling fans, lighting, and garage door openers; replaced light bulbs;
　　　and rewired light switches.

Custodian　　　　　　　　　　　　　　　　06/20xx to 03/20xx
First Bank Office Building, Wurzburg, Germany
Reference: Denise Powell. Phone: 320.555.5555
Hours per week: 5. Salary: $165 per month
  ▪ Cleaned a large office building with multiple offices, bathrooms, kitchen, front porch area,
　　　and stairwell.

EUROPEAN TRAVEL

Lived in Germany (12 years), and traveled to Italy, the Czech Republic, Austria, Poland, France,
and Egypt. Lived in a German farm village for two years, met German locals, and enjoyed the
culture.

Resume designed and edited by Diane Burns

Pursuing an Automotive Career with a Racing Team

Aaron Smith, age 20,
Associate degree student

Aaron has an eclectic background with experience in Web development, retail customer service, and automotive repair. Aaron applied to the CarTech vocational school as a junior in high school and took night and weekend classes, simultaneously with high school classes, to start working toward an early automotive degree. He began learning a wide array of automotive specialty skills. While in high school, he rebuilt a classic car and fell in love with car rebuilding and restoration.

His vocational training landed him a summer job in an automotive repair and remodeling shop as an apprentice, learning hands-on welding and automotive parts sales, applying his passion for custom-modeled cars to his everyday job. His starting pay was $25 per hour. He will apply to colleges during his second year to obtain a four-year degree in engineering to complement his automotive repair studies.

AARON SMITH

564 Constantine Road
Anaheim, CA 91913

714.555.5555
aasmith@hotmail.com

OBJECTIVE

Engineering Degree / Automotive

EDUCATION

Department of Defense General Adams High School, Wurzburg, Germany 09/20xx–06/20xx

- Attended Model United National Conference, Germany
- Served on a team that designed and launched the Department of Defense General Adams High School Web site — selected as first-place winner in region
- Varsity Football (Team Captain)

CarTech, Colorado 09/20xx–01/20xx

* The official technology school of NHRA
* Student Activities Council Representative

Completing coursework and certification in Specialized Automotive Technology with Chassis Fab & Management:

- Refrigerant Recovery & Recycling Review
- Drive Train Systems
- Chassis
- Basic Engine Management Systems
- Drivability Diagnostics
- All Data Information Specialist
- Certified Automatic Transmission Rebuilders (Qualified and Licensed through 2011 / Automatic Transmission Rebuilders Association)
- Race Team Technical Specialties

☐ **Motorsports Chassis Fabrication**
Engaged in hands-on instruction and internships specializing in metal working fabrication and techniques including MIG and TIG frame design and modifications including boxing, tubular cross-members, c-notching, pro-street frame setup, roll cage construction, and complete tube chassis fabrication. Laid out cut marks in preparation for cutting, drilling, or machining using oxy-acetylene and plasma; read and drew specialty mechanical drawings, operated grinder and sanders; applied attachment methods, metal finishing, and cutting. Demonstrated the care and usage of common precision measuring instruments for metal fabrication and machining.

☐ **Street Rod & Custom Fabrication & Custom Painting with Automotive Technology**
Customized vehicles and created works of art for street rods and custom fabrication. Used specialized sheet metal shaping fabrication techniques including chop tops, hidden pin hinges (suicide doors), and body construction including firewalls, floorboards, and transmission tunnels. Applied custom paint techniques including special effects, airbrushing, and pin striping as well as the application of specialized finishes. *Painted mailboxes and laptops for pay, while in school.*

Aaron Smith

☐ **Applied Service Management**
Learned business management concepts including finances, accounting, computers, and business applications.

EXPERIENCE

Custom Auto Body Technician / Mechanic   05/20xx–08/20xx
Hot Rod Shop, San Diego, CA
- Built a 1970 Firebird. Assembled and dissembled the vehicle to the frame. Removed the old drive train and assembled a new motor, transmission, and wiring harness. Removed rusted sheet metal. Custom upholstered seats and door panels. Installed power windows.

Owner/Manager   (Part-time) 03/20xx–02/20xx
Smith Website Design, Anaheim, CA
- Created a Website design business as a solution for online presence for small and medium-sized businesses, civic clubs, organizations, and churches. Used cutting-edge technology including Macromedia Studio MX 2004, Dreamweaver, Flash, Fireworks, and FreeHand, as well as Graphic Design, Flash, JavaScript, CGI, CSS, HTML, and (X)HTML.
- Designed and developed Web pages; provided computer service and support.

OTHER

- Lived in Germany, Korea, Japan, and Bahrain. Traveled to more than 35 countries.
- Special Olympics, Germany, Group Leader for Bowling Tournament.
- IT Skills: CISCO Networking I & II; LANs/WANs; MS Office Suite; Windows NT, XP, 2000.

Resume designed and edited by Diane Burns

Ronald Milestone, age 18, high school senior

Pursuing a BS in Construction Management

Ron Milestone volunteered one year to be a coordinator for construction projects for the local community. This was the beginning of his future career. Ron's paid positions involved lifeguarding and training children to swim, but he found that he enjoyed working with his hands and supervising projects. He continued to work with the construction committee and was successful in recruiting carpenters, electricians, sheetrock experts, painters, and other construction specialists to repair and upgrade various properties in the area. "I felt inspired to help people with improving the quality of their homes and businesses," he said.

Ronald Milestone

1456 E. Marion Street
Baltimore, MD 21204
Cell: 433-333-3333 ▪ milestone@md.edu

OBJECTIVE: Seeking an internship to gain professional experience in the construction industry.

EDUCATION

Towson Catholic High School, Towson, MD
Senior; expect to graduate in 20xx

WORK EXPERIENCE

Project Engineer Intern / Assistant   Summer 20xx
The Parson Contracting Company, Baltimore, MD

Worked as an assistant to a project engineer on a $55M construction project to build a visitor's center and underground parking garage.
- Interfaced daily with contractors, engineers, and other construction support professionals to review project status. Completed invoices and other administrative paperwork.
- Wrote and presented status reports at weekly project managers' meetings.
- Enhanced skills in problem resolution, project management, and cost management.

Manager, Park Swim Club, Towson, MD   May 20xx to August 20xx

Promoted to Manager within two weeks. Supervised 17 lifeguards. Developed weekly work schedules for all employees. Maintained safe environment for patrons by enforcing club rules and regulations.
- Learned to effectively mediate and satisfy customer concerns.
- Acquired leadership and crew management skills. Selected as Lifeguard of the Year.

Lifeguard, Hawaii Park Center, Outdoor Recreation, Honolulu, HI   July 20xx to January 20xx

Performed and assisted with water rescue and situations. Patrolled the harbor. Performed beach maintenance. Received an Aloha Award for customer service.

ACTIVITIES / VOLUNTEER SERVICE

Habitat for Humanity   September 20xx to Present
- Participate in community service construction projects

Salvation Army   January 20xx to Present
- Gain community service credits helping to sort and process donated items.

SKILLS

- Knowledge of construction principles, basic building systems, and project management.
- Strong problem solving, teamwork, leadership, and project management skills.
- Computer Skills: Proficient in Word, Excel, and PowerPoint; 4-D, AutoDesk Revit, Microsoft Project, and OnScreen Takeoff. Ability to use Excel to assist with takeoffs and cost management.

Resume designed and edited by Carla Waskiewicz

Michelle Marton, age 23,
college senior

Pursuing a Peace Corps Assignment

Michelle Marton is committed to pursuing economic and social justice through her coursework, volunteer work, and work experience. In the summer of her freshman year of high school, she traveled to Vietnam, which included language skills and studying development in the third world. Michelle has taken every opportunity to share her enthusiasm and develop her skills across a broad spectrum of international, federal, state, local, and community activities.

Michelle's work experience includes two summers with a local police department and extensive tutoring of elementary students. She has had internships with Senate Majority Leader Richard Durbin, an environmental organization working with migrant workers in the Southwest under the sponsorship of the Ford Foundation, and a college professor working on a book. Her volunteer activities include the development of a local health fair that attracted more than 500 participants and support from more than 40 organizational sponsors, tutoring, and work with various groups such as Amnesty International and Get Out the Vote (GOTV).

Finally, on the academic front, Michelle has been involved in a number of school activities and has taken numerous honors and Advanced Placement courses. She is a member of the National Honor Society and has consistently been on the high school honor roll.

Michelle N. Marton

mmarton@abcmail.com
847.542.1234

PROFILE

Enthusiastic, hardworking college student with extensive volunteer experience at federal, city and local levels; committed to community involvement. Outstanding oral and written communication skills and proven ability to work with diverse communities and individuals. Polished, professional presentation; demonstrated success working both independently and in an office environment.

EDUCATION

University of Maryland, College Park, MD
      Bachelor of Arts, Education and Political Science, expected June 20xx

Green High School, Baltimore, MD, diploma 20xx
      Honor roll, National Honor Society, numerous honors and AP courses
      Active member of band, Green Club, Amnesty International

RELEVANT EXPERIENCE

Tutor, 20xx to present   Baltimore, MD
  Provide tutoring assistance and support to elementary students.

Intern, Summer 20xx   The Forest Guild, Sante Fe, NM
  Researched and wrote paper on Latino forestry workers in the American Southwest to fulfill Ford Foundation research grant. Prepared and delivered presentations throughout New Mexico to promote responsible and sustainable forest use. Outlined new methodology for incorporating socioeconomic data into community wildfire risk analysis.

Casework Intern, Summer 20xx   Office of Senator Richard J. Durbin, Chicago, IL
  Researched constituent issues, prepared written responses and provided information on a wide range of topics in response to constituent inquiries and concerns. Deputized registrar for GOTV.

Research Assistant, Summer 20xx   Northwestern University, Evanston, IL
  Researched and analyzed information from a wide variety of sources and conducted interviews with study participants on the success of junior college graduates for forthcoming book.

Chair and Secretary, 20xx–20xx   Project Prevent, Baltimore, MD
  Planned and organized community health fair for an underserved Baltimore community, which had more than 500 attendees. Solicited the participation of more than 40 health care organizations, publicity, food and other services.

Administrative Assistant, Summers 20xx, 20xx   Suburban Police Department, Catons, MD
  Provided a wide range of administrative support to police chief of 250+ officer force.

Resume designed and edited by Nancy Segal

Denise Giller, age 18,
high school senior

Pursuing an Early Childhood Development Degree and Education Certification Training

Denise is a go-getter. She started working as a volunteer in early childhood development while she was in middle school and progressed to a paid position during summer school in high school. She also had an internship with Sure Start, working with challenged elementary children during her senior year in high school. Because she was living overseas, she applied to several online universities and received several acceptance letters for consideration.

"I love working with children and especially children who have struggles. It feels really good to help them succeed with even the smallest of tasks...and see the smiles on their faces! I will complete my internship in the elementary school this year, and two credits will be applied to my college degree when I start college." Denise will further her education by applying to a graduate school after she obtains her undergraduate degree. She is seeking employment in a school district or group home to help pay for college.

DENISE R. GILLER

2398 Westbrook Way * Columbia, MD 21045
555.555.5555 *drg@yahoo.com

CAREER OBJECTIVE

Degree in Early Childhood Development to start a career helping young people with developmental disabilities to succeed in life.

EDUCATION, TRAINING & OTHER

Wurzburg American High School, Wurzburg, Germany, 20xx–20xx
- Honor Roll Student x 4 semesters
- Advanced Placement: English Literature
- Career Working Experience (Internship/see below)
- Friend's Club, Active Member (Boys and Girls Across America)
- Hinterbrand Challenge: One-week winter survival program in the Alps
- Cheerleading Captain (Wrestling)
- Drama: Actor, Singer, Dancer (*Sly Fox* and *Guys and Dolls*)
- Homecoming Committee
- Spirit Club

Computer Skills
- Software Applications 1 and 2; PowerPoint, Excel, Word, Office, Access, and Publisher
- Typing: 60 + WPM
- Internet (research, AIM, set up and manage e-mail accounts)

Community, Retail, and High School Training: Sure Start and Pre-School Child Development Training, 20xx (40 hours of training), Department of Defense Dependent Schools Seminar (Certified as a Sure Start Aide); Anti-Terrorist Training, 20xx (online certification); AAFES Training, 20xx (Customer Service), 8 hours; Concessionaire Training, 20xx (Customer Service), 3 hours

High School Internships: Career Working Experience, Teacher's Aide, Sure Start, Wurzburg Elementary School 20xx; Career Working Experience, Teacher's Aide, Middle School Language Arts (Inclusions/Remedial), 20xx

EXPERIENCE

SURE START AIDE
U.S. Department of Defense Dependent Schools, Wurzburg, Germany   Summers and Sr. Year
Internship 20xx to 20xx
- Assisted one teacher with 18 students ages 4 and 5 in a Sure Start program providing specialized developmental care and instruction to contribute to their social, emotional, intellectual, and physical development. Worked closely with students to develop self-help skills/motor skills (using scissors, pouring milk, riding bikes, using eating utensils). Coached the development of manners and social etiquette (including eating and personal hygiene). Taught students basic counting and numbers, colors, letters, reading skills, and computer use.

- Participated in home visits prior to school to meet the children and their parents to assess their personalities and needs. Maintained confidentiality of school-related matters and monitored students' academic needs and social behavior. Maintained each child's work folders during the school year. Observed the students' behavior and activities and reported to the teacher as required for the development of progress reports.

- Sat in parent/caregiver conferences. Observed students for signs of illness, abuse, or neglect. Provided the teacher with remarks for appropriate assessments regarding children's behavior and activities, both negative and positive. Interacted with parents on a regular basis to report student progress and behaviors. Supervised and monitored children on the playground, on field trips, in restrooms, and at lunch and bus loading areas. Participated in games and activities.

- Designed and decorated Sure Start bulletin boards. Managed administrative requirements: Set out mats for naps, cleaned the room and organized supplies, set up and cleaned lunch tables, and filled out medical/accident forms. Operated school automation equipment.

LEARNING IMPAIRED AIDE
Wurzburg Elementary School, Leighton Barracks, Germany   10/20xx to 06/20xx

- Served as a Learning Impaired Aide floater supervising 15 students. Supervised handicapped students ages 5 to 10 with specific disabilities/needs, i.e., autism and mental handicaps (mild to moderately impaired students requiring a resource or self-contained setting as appropriate). Facilitated artwork, math, puppets, and reading activities. Observed student behavior and reported to the appropriate teacher in writing for inclusion in progress reports.

- Quickly responded to students and provided a calming influence when they acted out (kicking other children, throwing a tantrum, screaming, biting, hitting, etc.). Supervised students during field trips. Enforced and upheld school regulations and discipline.

- Created bulletin boards, wrote worksheets and workbooks, and operated the copier machine. Assisted the teacher in preparing instructional materials for class lessons. Distributed and collected items including tests, homework assignments, and classroom handouts.

OTHER

- Mission Trip—worked one-on-one with 12-year-old students (who only spoke Spanish) for ministry work, and assisted doctors in the medical clinic, 20xx
- Community Fest, Volunteer Worker, 20xx
- Certified Babysitter including CPR, Super Babysitting Course, Columbia, Teen Center, 20xx
- Student of Piano—completed 6th year
- Lived in Germany from ages 3 to 12 and 16 to 18 and traveled to 12 countries

Resume designed and edited by Diane Burns

Majoring in English Toward a Career in Marketing and Public Relations

Thomas Garner, age 17, high school senior

In high school, Tom really didn't know what he wanted to do after graduation. During the summer months, he held a variety of odd jobs ranging from construction laborer to working in a warehouse. In high school, Tom did well in English and liked to write. He really enjoyed contributing to his high school newspaper. He was also very creative and became interested in the idea of marketing a business.

During his senior year, he was awarded a scholarship to the University of Maryland. He plans to major in English. He hopes to apply for summer internships in marketing and public relations. This will give him the chance to be creative, use his writing skills, and gain job experience in his area of interest.

THOMAS GARNER

7290 Homewood Ct.
garner@yahoo.com • College Park, MD 20740 • (410) 888-8098

ACADEMIC GOAL: To attend a college or university with a strong English or Public Relations program and to pursue internships in public relations.

EDUCATION

Tolbert Hall High School, Towson, Maryland
Expect to graduate in 20xx

Academic Honors:	Peer Tutor (English Tutoring Program), McMullen Program (4-year honors program with culminating "thesis" style project). AP Courses (English, History). Top 10% of class. National Merit Scholar Honorable Mention.
Athletics:	JV and Varsity Football; All MIAA Senior year Basketball and Rugby (Freshman/Sophomore) Nominee for "Scholar Athlete" for National Football Foundation (20xx)
Activities:	Big Brothers Mentoring Program; French Club; Contributing Writer, School Newspaper

WORK EXPERIENCE

Banquet Server, May 20xx–Present, Martin's, Westminster, MD
• Provided hospitality service at special events held at major hotels in the Baltimore area.

Laborer, Martin Sampson Concrete Co. Inc., June 20xx–August 20xx
• Worked 65- to 80-hour weeks doing concrete construction in and around the Baltimore area.
• Learned various construction techniques including some carpentry and masonry skills.

Warehouse Assistant, Odyssey School, June 20xx–August 20xx
• Assembled and packaged lesson plans for home schooling programs.

SUMMARY OF RELEVANT SKILLS

- Very strong writing, oral communications, and presentation skills.
- Excellent research, analytical, and critical-thinking skills.
- Service-motivated with keen interest in humanitarian services.
- Computer: Proficient in Microsoft Office (PowerPoint, Excel, Word), Adobe Acrobat, ACT! 2000, FDP Contact Partner, Lexis-Nexis, Factiva, Bacons/Cision, Google AdWords, Yahoo! Sponsored Search, Omniture; Experience with QDA Miner, Smart Office 5, Adobe Photoshop Elements 5.0.
- Language: Basic writing and conversational skills in French.

Resume designed and edited by Carla Waskiewicz

Pursuing a Degree in Business

*Matthew Manowitz, age 17,
high school junior*

Matthew Manowitz had this to say about his future plans: "My school and summer activities and my part-time job revolve around golf. I love the game, the people, and the business. I hope someday to be involved in the golf industry in sales, management, or some other aspect of the sport. I would like to continue to play golf in college. I am sending my resume directly to golf coaches for their review. I know I must be realistic, though, because landing a spot on a college golf team is very competitive. My top priority, really, is to gain admission to a college with a strong business program."

MATTHEW C. MANOWITZ

25065 Triadelphia Mill Road • Ellicott City, Maryland 21117
(410) 444-3333 • Email: manowitz@net.net

Academic Goal:

To attend a college or university with a strong Business Administration program focusing on International Business.

Athletic Goal:

To utilize my experience and strong background in competitive junior golf to become a member of a college/university golf team.

Skills Summary:

Articulate and responsible	Proficient in Word and PowerPoint
Enthusiastic team player	Enjoy new challenges
Excellent public speaking skills	Strong interpersonal skills

Education:

Mount St. Joseph High School, Baltimore, Maryland
Junior; expect to graduate May 20xx
College Preparatory Classes—Full honors curriculum 20xx to 20xx. Courses include French II & III, Chemistry, Geometry, Language Arts, and World History.

Golf Achievements:

More than five years of experience competing in area junior golf in tournaments, including two years in the Titleist Junior Tour, PGA Middle Atlantic Section. Experienced in stroke play and match play. Current USGA Handicap: 7.9. Lowest 18-hole score: 74. Average 18-hole score: 80.

- **Sophomore Year,** 20xx–20xx
  Varsity Golf Team, position 5/6 on a 10-man team.

- **Freshman Year,** 20xx–20xx
  JV Golf Team, position 2/3 on a 7-man team. **MIAA Champions, 20xx.**

Other Sports / Extracurricular Activities:

Junior Varsity Track Team, 2 years
Recreational Team Basketball, 6 years
Volunteer Coach for youth basketball program, 2 years

Employment:

Caddy & Bag Room Assistant
Hunt Valley Golf Club, Ellicott City, Maryland   Summers 20xx & 20xx

Recommendations: Upon request

Resume designed and edited by Carla Waskiewicz

*Karen Johnson, age 17,
high school senior*

Pursuing a College Degree in Education

Karen has been dancing since she was a child. She is passionate about drama and dance, appearing in many local jazz recitals in the Atlanta area and a number of productions at her high school. She has worked closely with the head of the drama department. In fact, she has been involved in choreographing every high school production in the last two years.

Above all, Karen loves working with young people. As a camp counselor she has had the opportunity to directly affect the lives of many in a positive fashion. Her leadership capabilities were widely recognized. She was selected to return each year to the camp, each time progressing to a more senior counselor level and with added responsibility.

Karen leads by example with her strength of character and commitment. She volunteers with her faith-based community in a number of activities throughout the Atlanta area, including Habitat for Humanity. She welcomes the opportunity and responsibility to mentor those younger than her. Karen's strong work ethic coupled with her drive and commitment will definitely be an asset as she pursues a degree in education.

Karen Marie Johnson

1110 Club Circle
Atlanta, Georgia
30319

(404) 555-1212
email@email.com

Profile

Accomplished student skilled in choreography, dance and other theatre arts disciplines. Exceptional interpersonal and leadership skills.

Education

Parker High School, Atlanta, Georgia
High School Diploma, expected June 20xx
- General College Preparatory Curriculum
- Advanced Placement: AP Art History, AP Economics

Experience

Camp Counselor—YMCA Camp Blue Lagoon
- Create and lead activities designed to build character and sense of social responsibility for 63 campers ages 8–13.
- Instruct and motivate young campers in the areas of dance and drama.
- Excelled through leadership ranks over 3 years.

Choreographer—High School Theatre Productions
- Selected as Student Assistant to Department Head.
- Choreographed 7 production numbers for spring musicals.
- Appeared in 3 high school musicals.
- Mentored 3 underclassmen.

Activities

Peer Leader and Retreat Leader
- Chosen to represent Parker High School in orienting new students to the Parker environment and fostering a sense of community.

Peace by Piece Representative
- Chosen as one of only 12 students to represent the Christian religion in this faith-based alliance. This organization is designed to teach awareness and tolerance to high school students. Other religions represented include Judaism and Islam.

Other Activities

Varsity Swimming, Atlanta Jazz Theatre Dance Company, Youth Counselor Methodist Church, Babysitting Service

Resume designed and edited by Sharon M. Bowden

Pursuing a College Degree in International Affairs and Environmental Awareness

*Molly Jackson, age 17,
high school senior*

Molly Jackson believes in making a difference. Her exceptional academic ability has provided her with opportunities to share her interest in different cultures with travels as a People to People Ambassador. Her four years (since eighth grade) taking Japanese as a foreign-language elective was very beneficial. Although she is not totally fluent, her attempt and desire to communicate brought smiles to many faces as she spent time with the people of Japan.

Not only does Molly excel academically, but she has also demonstrated her leadership in both the athletic and volunteer arenas. As an avid swimmer, she has successfully coached many young children over the past two years with her job as an assistant swim coach. During the school year she has served as president of the Environmental Club and as an Ambassador internationally as well as locally within her school. Perhaps most notable is her selection to the Athletic Leadership Council, which promotes good sportsmanship, integrity on and off the field, commitment, and teamwork.

Molly also loves art. She participated in an internship program allowing her to experience firsthand the world of work. Serving as an assistant photographer and preparing educational materials at the nature center were great opportunities. Her role as an ambassador, internships, volunteer activities, and work experiences along with her academic achievements will serve her well as she pursues her college search.

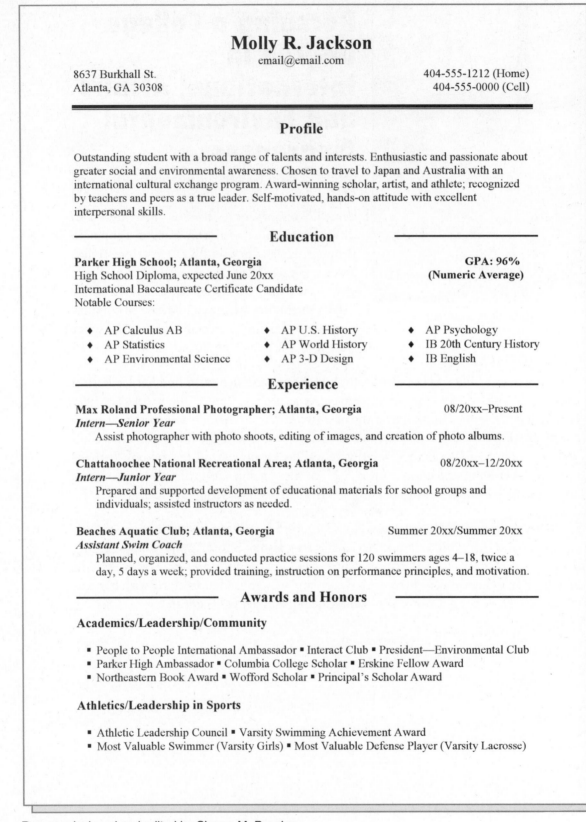

Molly R. Jackson

email@email.com

8637 Burkhall St.   404-555-1212 (Home)
Atlanta, GA 30308   404-555-0000 (Cell)

Profile

Outstanding student with a broad range of talents and interests. Enthusiastic and passionate about greater social and environmental awareness. Chosen to travel to Japan and Australia with an international cultural exchange program. Award-winning scholar, artist, and athlete; recognized by teachers and peers as a true leader. Self-motivated, hands-on attitude with excellent interpersonal skills.

Education

Parker High School; Atlanta, Georgia   **GPA: 96%**
High School Diploma, expected June 20xx   **(Numeric Average)**
International Baccalaureate Certificate Candidate
Notable Courses:

- AP Calculus AB
- AP Statistics
- AP Environmental Science
- AP U.S. History
- AP World History
- AP 3-D Design
- AP Psychology
- IB 20th Century History
- IB English

Experience

Max Roland Professional Photographer; Atlanta, Georgia   08/20xx–Present
Intern—Senior Year
   Assist photographer with photo shoots, editing of images, and creation of photo albums.

Chattahoochee National Recreational Area; Atlanta, Georgia   08/20xx–12/20xx
Intern—Junior Year
   Prepared and supported development of educational materials for school groups and individuals; assisted instructors as needed.

Beaches Aquatic Club; Atlanta, Georgia   Summer 20xx/Summer 20xx
Assistant Swim Coach
   Planned, organized, and conducted practice sessions for 120 swimmers ages 4–18, twice a day, 5 days a week; provided training, instruction on performance principles, and motivation.

Awards and Honors

Academics/Leadership/Community

- People to People International Ambassador ▪ Interact Club ▪ President—Environmental Club
- Parker High Ambassador ▪ Columbia College Scholar ▪ Erskine Fellow Award
- Northeastern Book Award ▪ Wofford Scholar ▪ Principal's Scholar Award

Athletics/Leadership in Sports

- Athletic Leadership Council ▪ Varsity Swimming Achievement Award
- Most Valuable Swimmer (Varsity Girls) ▪ Most Valuable Defense Player (Varsity Lacrosse)

Resume designed and edited by Sharon M. Bowden

Monica River, age 18, high school senior

Pursuing Athletic Scholarships

Monica River is sending this resume to college women's lacrosse coaches for full athletic scholarships. Many juniors in high school have already verbally committed to the school they intend to play for. Some even commit in the fall of the senior year. Keeping a close record of athletic events, sports, and scores is critical to landing a full athletic scholarship with a college.

Monica S. River
1010 Holmehurst Avenue
Catonsville, Maryland 21228
410-444-4444   msriver@aol.com

OBJECTIVE: To obtain a college degree from a top Women's Lacrosse University

SCHOLASTIC: 20xx Graduate of <u>Mount De Sales Academy</u>, Baltimore, Maryland
GPA: 2.5 (w/MDS grading scale)   SAT: 1080 (Verbal: 520, Math: 560), PSAT: Verbal: 51, Math: 55

<u>**LACROSSE BACKGROUND:**</u> Position: MIDFIELD/CENTER

<u>**Senior Year:**</u> Started as a full field A-Wing on team which finished 9-8. Personal Stats: 31 goals (2nd on team), 8 assists (3rd), 37 Gr. Balls (2nd). *Club Team:* Sky walkers 'xx Blue. *Tournaments:* USTC Fall 'xx, U of Maryland Challenge Cup Fall 'xx. *Summer 'xx:* Metro Open League, Baltimore, Md. *Fall 'xx:* Checkhers League, Eldersburg, Md.
<u>**Junior Year:**</u> Played D-Wing/3rd Man behind restraining line on team which finished 14-4-4 and won an IAAM A League Divisional Title. Personal Stats: 3 Goals, 16 Gr. Balls. *Club Teams:* Sky walkers 'xx Blue, M&D Lax. *Camps:* Maryland Super Elite at Bryn Mawr, North Carolina Elite, Loyola Elite 300. *Tournaments:* National Draw 'xx, All Star Express 'xx, USTC Fall 'xx, U of Maryland Challenge Cup Fall 'xx, Turkey Shoot Fall 'xx. *Summer 'xx:* Metro Open League, Baltimore, Md. *Fall 'xx:* Checkhers League, Eldersburg, Md.
<u>**Sophomore Year:**</u> Started as the full field D-Wing on squad that won the IAAM JV A League. *Team record:* 15-2. *Personal Stats:* 30 Goals (3rd on team), 30 Gr. Balls (3rd). Named Most Improved Player. Scored game-winning goals vs. St. Mary's Annapolis (4-3) and Notre Dame Prep (13-12). *Club Teams:* Baltimore Lady Lax, ROME. *Camps:* Loyola Elite 300, Duke Super Elite. *Tournaments:* National Draw 'xx, All Star Express 'xx, Ocean City Lax Fest 'xx, Quick Stix Fall Turkey Shoot 'xx. *Summer 'xx:* Metro League, Baltimore, Md.
<u>**Freshman Year:**</u> Played full field A-Wing on squad in IAAM JV A League. Team record 11-4. *Camps:* U of Maryland Elite, McDonogh Attack Camp. *Summer 'xx:* Metro League, Baltimore, Md.

<u>**OTHER ATHLETIC BACKGROUND:**</u> Earned 10 Total Varsity Letters

<u>**Senior Year:**</u> *Varsity Cross Country:* Team finished #10 in Baltimore area. 5K time: 21:03. *Varsity Indoor Track:* Captain of team that won IAAM Championship, ranked #3 in Baltimore area. Named to *Baltimore Sun* All-Met Indoor Track Team. Named to All-Maryland State Private School Indoor Track Team. Named to *Baltimore Sun* All-County/-City Indoor Track Team. Named to IAAM All-Star Team. Championship results: 1st in 55 dash, 1st in long jump, 2nd in 55 hurdles, 2nd in triple jump. Named MVP of team.
<u>**Junior Year:**</u> *Varsity Cross Country:* Team finished #5 in Baltimore area. 5K time: 20:26. *Varsity Indoor Track:* Team won IAAM Championship, ranked #5 in Baltimore area. Named to All-Maryland State Private School Team. Named to IAAM All-Star Team. Championship results: 1st in 55 hurdles, 2nd in 300 dash, 3rd in 55 dash. Set school record for most points/season.
<u>**Sophomore Year:**</u> *Varsity Cross Country:* Team finished #8 in Baltimore area. 5K time: 20:29. *Varsity Indoor Track:* Team won IAAM Championship, ranked #10 in Baltimore area. Named to *Baltimore Sun* All-County/-City Indoor Track Team. Named to All-Maryland State Private School Indoor Track Team. Named to IAAM All-Star Team. Championship results: 1st in 55 hurdles, 2nd in high jump, 1st in 4 × 400 relay (anchor), 6th in 55 dash. Named MVP of team.
<u>**Freshman Year:**</u> *Varsity Cross Country:* Team ranked #10 in Baltimore area. 5K time: 21:15. *Varsity Indoor Track:* Events 55 hurdles, high jump, 4 × 400 relay.

WORK HISTORY: Lifeguard, 4 years

Height: 5' 6"
Weight: 123 lbs.
Age: 18, Right-Handed
Health: Excellent
40-yd. Time: 5.37 seconds
50-yd. Time: 6.68 seconds

Applications, Cover Letters, and Additional Job Search Materials

In some cases, you are not finished with the entire application by submitting just a resume. With employment and internship opportunities, as well as college applications, you will probably have to complete an application (often online), answer essay questions, and write a personal statement. You also need to send a cover letter. College, job, internship, co-op, work-study, and workshop opportunities are very competitive, and recruiters and admissions committees ask for more information from you than just a resume in many cases. You will have to follow the directions, take the time to complete the full application, write your narratives, and submit it all correctly.

In many cases, the application process is a test to see how well you follow directions. If you can't follow the directions and complete the entire application, you will not be considered for the opportunity.

This chapter introduces you to the additional materials you might need to include with your resume, such as job applications, questionnaires, essays and narratives, cover letters, thank-you letters, and reference lists.

Application Forms

Many internship, job, and work-study applications are posted online. To manage the volume of applicants, student recruiters ask for more information than just a resume. They might ask for a complete application form, which often asks about your skills and experience in relation to the job or internship and your interests in this opportunity. Follow the directions carefully: This is a test.

Job application forms can be annoying, but recruiters and managers like to see the information organized in a consistent way so that they can find the information they seek. You have to be patient and complete the forms. But you can usually attach your resume to most applications in some way. It's best to actually fill out the form, in addition to attaching the resume.

Remember when filling out applications to do the following:

- Use only the space allowed for descriptions of work experiences. If the space is small, keep your descriptions short. If you need to include longer descriptions, attach your resume.

- Fill in all the blanks. If they ask for supervisors or references, be sure to add them. Keep a list of references, phone numbers, and e-mail addresses available for applications.

- Include your educational activities and honors. Usually you can add these into an "other information" field toward the end of the application.

- Write a short statement in the "other information" field about why you would like to have this position and the skills you can bring to the job; or attach a cover letter including this information.

- Proofread to make sure there are no typos.

- Be consistent with writing style, capitalization, and grammar.

- Follow the directions for attachments.

Now all you have to do is be patient. This job could be yours if the application is well done and you have followed the directions. The application is an employment examination. If it's sloppy, incomplete, or inaccurate, you will not get an interview or consideration for the job.

Questionnaires and Essays

The questions in the following sample application are basically interview questions. The employer is giving you a chance to think about working for them and what would be most important in doing that. Your answers to these questions, plus your resume, decide whether you'll get an actual interview for a position.

Questions and narrative answers are becoming an important part of the job application process today. Hiring managers and recruiters can read your answers and decide whether they like your writing and critical-thinking skills.

The following are tips for writing the best narrative answers to questionnaires:

- Be sure to answer the question.

- If you're applying for a job or internship, study the company's mission to become very familiar with its services and customers. If you're applying for admission to college, look at the philosophy of the college and make sure you mention that you have a similar philosophy and educational goal.

- Give examples of your own academic or other experience that demonstrate your interest in the job.

- Pick out the important keywords from the question. Use those keywords in your answer, to make sure you have answered it correctly in the language of the company or college.

- Use the personal pronoun "I" with your answer because these are personal narrative statements.

- Add enthusiasm, energy, congeniality, and motivation to your answers. A positive attitude is impressive, winning, engaging, and attention getting.

- Proofread, edit, and make sure the answers are written well. This is actually a writing and critical-thinking test.

- Have someone else read the questions and answers to make sure the answers are well written and not too long.

Following are some example application questions and answers:

1. **Have you ever visited a Cool Beans store? How was it?** Yes, I love Cool Beans; it's my favorite coffee store, especially near the holidays when I can get the seasonal Christmas hot chocolate! I think that the baristas work hard, but have a good time with their work responsibilities and ensuring that customers are taken care of with the best, friendliest service.

2. **Do you drink coffee?** I am a coffee drinker. I especially like caffè e latti and espresso.

3. **Why do you want to work here?** I would like to be a barista and team member where I can get to know the coworkers, provide high-quality service, manage inventory efficiently, and communicate with customers quickly and with concern.

4. **Tell about a time when you have provided good customer service.** My family's grocery store is a neighborly kind of store that people come back to frequently. Customers look for particular items, and I made sure we had these

items for their meals. I have frequently gathered items for family members who could not come to the store. I delivered these items to their homes. In fact, I delivered during bad weather, snow, and rain, so that some customers didn't have to leave their homes.

College, Scholarship, or Internship Essays

Your college application essay is an important narrative about your interest in the school and your background. College recruiters look for well-written narratives about candidates' experiences that will contribute to the success of those candidates at their colleges.

When writing college entrance essays, do the following:

- Write the truth.
- Give dates and a reference for your examples (in case the reader doesn't have your resume).
- Tell a story or give an anecdote about yourself.
- Write about the lessons you have learned.
- Write about something you are proud of in your high school career.
- Write about challenges that you overcame and how you overcame them.
- Write about your vision for yourself as a college student and your future career.
- Have someone edit and proofread your narrative.
- Write in first person—use the personal pronoun "I."
- Follow the narrative length and application instructions carefully.
- This is a writing test, so consider this a significant research paper.

The following is an example of an essay topic and an appropriate response. Review it to see what this applicant did right. Also, consider responding to the topic yourself with your own essay for practice.

Topic: How I have grown and changed since my freshman year of high school and the experiences that have fostered my development as a person.

My first year at Mount St. Joseph High School was a very difficult one for me. I felt very lost and alone. All of my close friends had chosen to attend another high school. I knew only one other student in my freshman class. I chose St. Joe's because I knew it was the best fit for me, but I doubted my choice during the first few months of my freshman year because the transition seemed overwhelming.

As a freshman, I was very afraid to take risks and to be a leader. I found myself following the crowd and making choices that others would accept, not necessarily the best ones for me. I had a difficult time adjusting to my tough schedule of all honors courses. I tried out for the basketball team and was not chosen. But I was determined to turn things around. In the spring of my freshman year, I was successful in making the JV golf team, which proved to be a turning point for me. The person I am today is a result of personal success and growth, as well as my failures. My participation on the golf team helped me to develop patience and persistence, and to be positive, win or lose.

This year, I was one of 20 students chosen to participate in a weeklong service project in a very poor community in rural Virginia. Our job for the week was to repair homes and clean up the community. The residents' homes were in terrible shape and did not even have indoor plumbing. I was in utter shock to learn that in an area so close to my home, there are people who cannot afford indoor plumbing.

The week I spent in Cape Charles proved to be one of the most significant experiences of my life. It helped me realize how much I take for granted in my life and how important it is to help others. The people were so appreciative of our help. Even though they were very poor, they were also very generous, and they offered to share what little they did have with our group. This amazing experience not only affected my personal outlook on life but reinforced my commitment to community service.

As a freshman, I hesitated to be a leader and to make my own decisions for fear of what my peers might say. As a senior preparing to meet a whole new set of risks and challenges, I feel I have learned a lot from my high school experiences. My participation in school sports, clubs, leadership programs, and community service has influenced how I see the world and how I interact with others. It has also helped me to become a better person. Today, I am more self-confident and not afraid to take risks. I consider myself a leader rather than a follower and I am more committed to helping others.

Essay Worksheet

Try responding to the preceding sample essay topic yourself. Use the sample answer to help guide you in how to appropriately answer; however, be certain to personalize what you say.

_____

_____

_____

_____

_____

_____

_____

_____

_____

_____

_____

_____

Persuasive Cover Letters

Today, cover letters can be on paper or delivered as e-mail. The content is about the same either way. Today's hiring and human resources managers are very busy. You have only a few seconds to impress them. Your cover letter is another opportunity to pitch your interest, skills, and qualifications for the position.

In your cover letter, summarize the best of what you have to offer. The goals of the cover letter are the following:

- Get the reader's attention.
- Impress the employer.
- Use keywords and skills from the recruitment ad.
- Show your genuine interest in the company and its customers.
- Show that you are enthusiastic, energetic, dependable, professional, and determined.

Use the cover letter to highlight experiences that are of interest to the employer. You can highlight an important accomplishment, such as being a champion swimmer, playing a main role in the school play, or pitching for the school's baseball team. Potential employers will see you as a person with energy and enthusiasm. Hopefully, they will want to meet you and see whether you have the same enthusiasm in person.

A good cover letter should contain seven sections:

1. Your contact information

2. The employer's contact information

3. Greeting

4. Intro paragraph

5. Middle paragraph with important skills

6. Closing paragraph with logistics information

7. Signature and attachments

Following is a description and sample for each section.

Your Contact Information

Start your cover letter with your name, your contact information, and the date. Use the same format and fonts you used in your resume.

KALIN C. SMYTHE
4404 Allison Drive / Baltimore, MD 21229
(410) 999-9999 / kalincsmythe@net.com

The Employer's Contact Information

Personalize the letter with the hiring manager's name if you can. Otherwise, you can write *Attention: Barista Recruiter.*

COOL BEANS CORPORATION
Student Recruitment Division
Attention: Aglaope Singerman, Barista Recruiter
2000 Bucks Drive
Seattle, WA 20202

Salutation

There are three ways to address the sender. If you know the person's gender, begin the letter with the appropriate title and surname preceded by "Dear."

> Dear Mr. Walters:

If you don't know whether this person is a man or a woman, begin the letter with something like this.

> Dear M. Walters:

If no name is listed in the job advertisement, begin the letter like this.

> Dear Recruiter:

Opening Paragraph

Following are four types of opening paragraphs. Choose the one that matches how you learned about the position. Study it to help you write your own opening paragraph.

Openers for Responding to Online Job Listings

An online application could include a cover letter attached to an e-mail, written as text in the e-mail, or text pasted into an "Other Information" field. Keep the message short and to the point. Following is a sample opening paragraph.

> Subject: **KALIN C. SMYTHE**, Applicant, Barista, Seattle, WA
>
> **KALIN C. SMYTHE**
> 4404 Allison Drive / Baltimore, MD 21229
> (410) 999-9999 / kalinsmythe@net.com
>
> Dear Barista Recruiter,
>
> I am completing your online application for the position of barista.

Openers for Responding to Newspaper Ads

You might find a job advertisement in your local newspaper or similar publication. If so, use an opening paragraph like the following.

> **KALIN C. SMYTHE**
> 4404 Allison Drive / Baltimore, MD 21229
> (410) 999-9999 / kalinsmythe@net.com
>
> June 15, 20XX
>
> Dear Barista Recruiter,
>
> I found your recruitment ad on indeed.com. I am submitting my application for the position of barista.

Openers for Responding to Referrals

Referrals and leads from friends and family members are great! Be sure to mention the referrer's name in the opening paragraph.

> Subject: **KALIN C. SMYTHE**, Interested in Barista Position
>
> Dear Ms. Singerman,
>
> I was referred to you by my friend Jason Sparks, who works in your downtown location. He speaks very highly of the employee-friendly work environment there and thinks I would be a good addition to the team.

Openers for Initiating Direct Contact

It's easy to research contacts and obtain e-mail addresses through the Internet. Without any introduction, you might write directly to someone who works in a company or agency. You can write an e-mail with an introduction similar to the following.

> Subject: **KALIN C. SMYTHE**, Interested in Your Company
>
> Dear Ms. Singerman,
>
> I found your information while researching your company. I would like to apply for an internship or entry-level position with Cool Beans. I'm interested in gaining more information about your opportunities. I have attached my resume with my educational background and work experience. I would appreciate any information you can give me about opportunities with Cool Beans.

Middle Paragraph with Best Skills

You might find a job advertisement in your local newspaper or similar publication. If so, use a middle paragraph like the following.

> I am a junior in high school and have retail experience. I would like to be a member of a barista team in the Seattle area. My important skills for this position include the following:
>
> - I love coffee and have a good memory for complex orders.
>
> - I am also fast-moving and efficient and can keep up with peak customer service times.

Closing Paragraph with Contact Info

Write some details about your availability, including your ability to get to work. You can mention your interest in number of hours, but be flexible. This shows enthusiasm and willingness to work when you are needed most.

> I am available to work 20 hours per week, including weekends during the summer. I can also work flexible hours. I have a car, so my transportation is covered. [or: I can get to work by bus/metro from my home.] Thank you for your consideration. I hope to hear from you soon.

Signature and Enclosures

List any enclosures, such as a resume or recommendation letter, that you might be sending to the recruiter.

> Sincerely,
>
>
> **KALIN C. SMYTHE**
>
> Enclosure: resume

The Total Letter: Sample Referral Cover Letter

KALIN C. SMYTHE
4404 Allison Drive / Baltimore, MD 21229
(410) 999-9999 / kalinsmythe@net.com

Subject: **KALIN C. SMYTHE**, Interested in Barista Position

Dear Ms. Singerman,

I was referred to you by my friend Jason Sparks, who works in your downtown location. He speaks very highly of the employee-friendly work environment there and thinks I would be a good addition to the team.

I am a junior in high school and have retail experience. I would like to be a member of a barista team in the Seattle area. My important skills for this position include the following:

- I love coffee and have a good memory for complex orders.

- I am also fast-moving and efficient and can keep up with peak customer service times.

I am available to work 20 hours per week, including weekends during the summer. I can also work flexible hours. I have a car, so my transportation is covered. Thank you for your consideration. I hope to hear from you soon.

Sincerely,

KALIN C. SMYTHE

Enclosure: resume

Your Network

Who do you know? Don't keep your job, internship, or training program search a secret. Share your objectives with people who might know someone in the field. Talk to your parents, your relatives, and their friends about jobs or internship experiences that you might be suited for. E-mail or hand them your resume. Tell them what kind of experience you are interested in. Tell them where, when, and why you want to work. They need to clearly understand your objectives. Be specific. They will want to help you if you are clear about your objectives and availability.

Cover Letter Samples

The following cover letter was prepared by a student who was responding to an ad she saw on the Internet. The ad was for a library assistant position. Here's the ad, followed by the sample letter.

> **LIBRARY ASSISTANT—TECHNO TEEN.** HS student with computer skills needed to work with computers and library customers. Must know PCs, Word, Internet, and e-mail systems. Must be patient with nontechnical users. 20 hours/week. $10 per hour. Send resume and letter to Enoch Pratt Free Library, Baltimore, MD 21224, Attn: Ms. Carol Snyder. Or send by e-mail to carolsnyder@epfl.org.

Jennifer Holland
90909 Hollins Ferry Road
Arbutus, Washington 90909
Home: (909) 123-1234
Cell: (909) 999-9999
Email: Jennifer_holland121@yahoo.com

December 15, XXXX

King County Library System
15527 SE 8th St.
Bellevue, WA 98007

Dear Ms. Snyder:

Please find enclosed my resume for the position of Library Assistant, which I found listed on the Internet.

My relevant qualifications include the following:

- I have previously been a library page and have experience teaching the Techno Teens.
- I know the students and, more importantly, the work that will be required in the computer center.

I would be an asset to your organization because

- I can find books on the shelves twice as fast as the requirements.
- I am good at finding things that do not belong, such as books from other libraries.
- I have good people skills. I am patient with computers and people.
- I can solve computer problems very well.
- I am dependable and a hard worker.

I am available 20 hours per week. You can contact me at home after 3:00 most afternoons. Thank you for your interest. I look forward to your response.

Sincerely,

Jennifer Holland

Enc: Resume

The following cover letter was prepared by a student who was applying for a job at the hospital where her mother works. Her mother gave her the referral.

Reagan R. Ruhnke
3456 Rogers Ford Avenue
Columbia, MD 21045
Home: (301) 999-9999
Cell: (443) 999-9999
Email: Reagan_ruhnke@yahoo.com
July 26, XXXX

Ms. Dorothy Rogers, Human Resources
Howard County General Hospital
909 Bright Seat Road
Columbia, Maryland 90909

Dear Ms. Rogers:

I am submitting my resume for consideration for a part-time position as a Patient Services Representative. I know about the hospital positions and patient services through my mother, Kathryn Ruhnke, who has been a Registered Nurse in the emergency room for five years.

Please find enclosed my resume for the position of Patient Services Representative. My relevant qualifications include the following:
- I have been preparing for a job as a receptionist.
- I was in co-op during my senior year in high school.
- I was Co-op Student of the Month.
- I have worked as a receptionist at Career Connections, where I had various job duties such as helping visitors and answering the phone.
- I have also worked as a file clerk at Woman's Health.
- I worked for Landmark Staffing Agency for a year. I worked temporarily at several companies, as placed by Landmark.

I would be an asset to your organization because I am energetic, reliable, and cooperative. I want to be the best employee I can be. I am always on time to work. I am reliable, cooperative, and resourceful. I am willing to learn new things.

Thank you for your time and consideration. I look forward to hearing from you. I am available to begin working right away.

Sincerely,

Reagan R. Ruhnke
Enc: Resume

Sample Reference Lists

References are an important tool in your job search. Two good references will be enough for a recruiter or supervisor to check the quality of your work. Call and stay in contact with your references to keep up-to-date contact information and let them know that there might be contact from a potential employer or recruiter. Send them your resume occasionally to keep them up-to-date with your experiences and interest. This will help them give you a better reference because they will be more familiar with your activities.

Keep a separate sheet that lists your references and their contact information. You can give this list to an employer who asks for it. Following is an example of how this should look.

Kenny T. Day
1010 Edmondson Avenue
Louisville, KY 22222
(555) 444-4444

References

Janice J. Benjamin, President
New Options, Inc.
2311 E. Stadium, Suite B-2
Mount Washington, KY 22222
(555) 555-0000—Work
Supervisor, Internship, New Options, Summer XXXX

Jane Sommer, Director
Sports Management Department
Smith College
84 Elm Street
Frankfort, KY 22222
(555) 555-0000
Swimming coach, 5 years

Effective Thank-You Letters

You won't include a thank-you letter with your resume, obviously, but these documents are still integral to the application process. Do you want to be remembered after an interview? Sending a thank-you letter is the best way to accomplish this. The thank-you letter is a great opportunity to get your name in front of the interviewer again. You will have the chance to tell the person how much you appreciate his or her time and how much you like the organization. You can also reiterate that you would like to work for the interviewer's company.

This letter needs to be genuine. In the case of the barista interview, the applicant might write something like the following.

Dear Ms. Singerman,

Thank you for your introduction to the Cool Beans team yesterday. I believe I would fit in with the team as an excellent barista because of my ability to multitask, because I am friendly with customers, and because I have a good memory for orders. I am available to begin work next Monday.

Thanks again!

Sincerely,

KALIN C. SMYTHE

Employers like to know that you noticed their businesses, employees, and customers. When you're in an interview, pay attention to your surroundings. Find something you like and mention it in your thank-you letter.

 Write and e-mail your thank-you letter within 24 to 48 hours, while your interview is still fresh in your mind and in the employer's mind.

E-mail thank-you notes are very effective. The subject line should be

Thank You from [Your Name]

Always put your name in the subject line.

The letter itself might look something like the following.

> Dear Mr. Suites,
>
> Thank you very much for your time on Monday. I am very interested in your hotel management training program. I am available to begin work in two weeks. I look forward to hearing from you soon.
>
> Sincerely,
>
>
> Emily Nopolus

Manage Your Network

Create a file on your computer for network names, e-mails, phone numbers, job titles, companies, and how you know each person. Keep this network list for current and future job search possibilities and simply asking questions about any career topic. Your family members and friends will be very impressed with your researching of careers, companies, and opportunities. The information they provide could result in jobs, interviews, mentoring opportunities, and establishing excellent references.

What's Next?

In this chapter, you learned how to complete applications and create and save cover letters, reference lists, and thank-you letters. Your resume is your most important job search document, but these other three documents will also help you make a good impression on employers.

The final chapter of this book focuses on interviewing and other job search tips. You can see that applying for positions involves marketing, research, analysis, and writing. The result will be paid positions and career, job, training, and internship opportunities. Keep your resume up-to-date, so that you are ready for opportunities that could appear quickly. Act on chances to increase your skills and knowledge. The payoff with good jobs and training opportunities is worth your time in updating your resume and keeping track of references and your network.

Job, Internship, and College Interview and Search Tips

Now that your resume is finished, you are ready to research jobs or internships. There are three ways to find jobs or internships:

- Searching the Internet
- Walking in to a target business
- Talking to people you know

This chapter covers all of these options and gives you ideas on how to research opportunities.

Jobs vs. Internships

A job is important for earning money. An internship is important for gaining experience in a field that could become your future career.

The following is a list of some of the major differences between jobs and internships. You may have a choice between whether to get a job with a local business or apply for an internship that will give you particular skills and knowledge and a network in a certain industry.

Jobs	Internships
Paid.	Maybe paid, maybe volunteer.
Gain basic skills.	Gain specific skills for this industry.
Learn about an industry and company that could become part of your future.	Learn about an industry and company that could become part of your future.
Learn about customers in a specific field.	Learn about customers in a specific field.
Possibly learn something new depending on your skill level on entry.	Learn new things about a new industry or field of work.
May not add a potential reference or mentor.	May give you the opportunity to meet a reference, mentor, or expert who can guide you.
The organization may not be impressive for your future career.	May be impressive on the resume. Might help you get into college.

Job and Internship Worksheet

Can you think of other major differences between jobs and internships? Which would be right for you? Use the following lines to list some more differences.

Jobs	Internships
_____	_____
_____	_____
_____	_____
_____	_____

Internships, Co-ops, Work Studies, and Specialized Workshops

Whatever your special interest might be, there is probably an internship or other special program in this area. You will have to research your career field to find potential employers and open opportunities. The following sections explain how to do this.

If You Know Your Area of Internship Interest

You are lucky if you know what career you are interested in and what skills you hope to use in the future. If you know what career you want, you should definitely try to get work experience that relates to that career.

Find out about the companies in that field that are near where you live or want to live. First search the Web for companies. Then visit those companies' Web sites. Research their mission, services, and customers. Search for internships and entry-level, part-time, and summer opportunities.

If You Don't Know What Kind of Internship Is Best

You might not have decided on a specific career, but you still want to get experience that would be helpful to you. Think about what you like to do, including sports and school activities. Choose one related career that might interest you. By working in one field for the summer or on a part-time basis, you might determine whether a certain career is right for you.

See your guidance or career counselor at school for potential opportunities available to you. He or she will have a career and interest test that can help you identify your skills and interests. This kind of test can help you tremendously and give you great ideas about careers that might fit you.

Here are some ideas of the types of jobs you could search for, based on your current interests. They are grouped into 16 career "clusters" developed by the U.S. Department of Education.

- **01 Agriculture, Food & Natural Resources:** If you have a green thumb and enjoy working with plants, look for work at a landscaping firm, greenhouse, flower shop, gardening center, or tree farm. If you like animals, you could research animal hospitals, racetracks, pet stores, and grooming shops. You could google the following terms: High School, Internships, Landscaping, and the name of your city and state.

- **02 Architecture & Construction:** The construction industry is always growing and there are internship and part-time job opportunities for high school students. Good grades in math, computers, and arts courses could make a difference.

- **03 Arts, A/V Technology & Communications:** If you like the visual arts and A/V technology, you could look for work in an advertising agency, entertainment company, or movie production company. You could google the following terms: High School Internships, Arts & Entertainment, or Multimedia and the name of your city and state.

- **04 Business, Management & Administration:** If you enjoy business operations, you could find internships with local corporations. Search online for companies that interest you, and then search their Web sites for internships.

✏ **05 Education & Training:** If you like kids and have patience, you could look for a job at a daycare center, camp, or swimming pool. If you would like to be a speaker or instructor, begin working on your speaking skills wherever you can. You can find paid and volunteer positions in this area.

✏ **06 Finance:** If you like finance, accounting, and math, you could begin a great career in finance. You can find out about finance internships online. Your grades in math, statistics, and computers will make a difference.

✏ **07 Government & Public Administration:** Government agencies have student internship programs for high school students who are full-time and over the age of 16. Many are paid. You can find these internships at www.studentjobs.gov. These internships could convert into permanent positions.

✏ **08 Health Science:** If you have an interest in health and wellness, consider researching hospitals, nursing homes, assisted-living facilities, or physicians' offices. There are many positions for high school students to gain experience.

✏ **09 Hospitality & Tourism:** If you enjoy planning parties and school events, you could apply for positions with public relations firms, radio stations, hotels, or major sports teams.

✏ **10 Human Services:** If you like working with people—and if you have empathy to help children, families, and older people—you can find internships in human services. This way you can decide whether this career would work for you.

✏ **11 Information Technology:** Search for entry-level computer positions with other retailers or small businesses to get started and add IT experiences to your resume. You can search for entry-level IT positions on Craigslist (www.craigslist.org) or job Web sites.

✏ **12 Law, Public Safety, Corrections & Security:** If you want to work in public safety, you could look for positions with parks, volunteer fire departments, law firms, bonding agencies, or courts. You can look for government student internships by going to www.studentjobs.gov.

✏ **13 Manufacturing:** Look online to see whether there are manufacturing plants in your city or town. You can find entry-level positions or internships in many aspects of manufacturing that could help you begin a good career.

✏ **14 Marketing, Sales & Service:** If sales and marketing interest you, search for a job in sales, but realize you might not find an internship in marketing until college. Get started with a retail sales position.

✏ **15 Science, Technology, Engineering & Mathematics:** If you are interested in engineering or mathematics, determine which field interests you most. If geology is your favorite subject in science, look for an internship with a local natural-history museum. If you are interested in engineering, you might research manufacturing companies or other companies in your area that rely heavily on the skills of engineers.

- **16 Transportation, Distribution & Logistics:** Manufacturers all have to move their products from one location to another, on time and on budget. You could obtain an entry-level job or internship in planning transportation and distribution of products. This could be an excellent career.

Government Job and Internship Research Strategies

The following are some suggestions to research high school internships, co-ops, or work-study programs in government agencies:

- **Federal agencies or offices:** Research the agency of interest online. Then on the agency's Web site, search for high school internships. Read about the internship and write to the student recruiter online.

- **Military bases:** Your closest military base probably has high school jobs, internships, co-op programs, community service opportunities, and stay-in-school programs. If you know someone who works at the base, ask that person for a human resources representative's e-mail address so that you can write to them about high school internships. Or look up the military base online and look for civilian jobs or the name of the human resources representative.

To be eligible for a student appointment, you must

- Be at least 16 years old.

- Be enrolled or accepted for enrollment as a degree-seeking student.

- Be taking or be signed up to take at least a half-time academic, vocational, or technical course load.

- Be enrolled in or accepted for enrollment in an accredited high school, vocational school, two- or four-year college or university, or a graduate or professional school.

Internship Web Sites

Following are good sites to search for internship opportunities:

- **STUDENTJOBS.gov** (www.studentjobs.gov/e-scholar.asp): This Web site lists internship opportunities with the federal government. It gives descriptions and contact information for each internship and allows you to apply to the internship directly.

- **Intern Exchange International** (www.internexchange.com): This Web site links to a structured internship program in London, England. This program gives students the opportunity to work for top companies in England as well as provides students with a variety of different fields to explore, such as culinary arts and medicine.

✎ **The Princeton Review** (www.princetonreview.com/cte/search/ internshipAdvSearch.asp): The Princeton Review Web site allows high school students to customize a search for internships based on such factors as location, compensation, and the percentage of applicants who are selected for each internship.

✎ **Vault** (www.vault.com): Vault is an excellent resource for finding an internship because it offers a wide variety of internships and goes into detail describing each one. Not only that, but the Vault Web site ranks internships and provides advice as to which internships are the best to apply for. In addition, the site provides information on what it's like to work for certain employers.

✎ **CareerBuilder** (www.careerbuilder.com): CareerBuilder has many postings for internships. Students can upload their resumes and sign up for job alerts, which makes the process of finding an internship easier.

✎ **MonsterTrak** (www.monstertrak.com): Monster has a section devoted to internship advice that includes to-do lists for landing summer internships and help with determining which internships are right for you. Also, Monster has extensive listings of various internship opportunities in its internship database.

✎ **Internship Programs.com** (http://internshipprograms.com/home.asp): This Web site is very user friendly and allows students to upload their resumes to employers who are looking exclusively for interns. Also, the site has a good selection of various internships.

✎ **Quintessential Careers** (www.quintcareers.com/teen_jobs.html): This part of the Quintessential Careers site is tailored to teens and provides great links for people in high school looking for internships. Not only that, but the site allows students to do advanced job searches and have listings e-mailed to them.

✎ **idealist.org** (www.idealist.org/if/as/Internship): Idealist is a great site to search for internships—especially in the nonprofit sector. The site even has a section devoted to helping students learn what they need to do to break into nonprofits.

✎ **icouldbe.org** (www.icouldbe.org/standard/default.asp): icouldbe.org provides career mentors to teens. The mentors on the site work directly with teens to help them plan their careers and find job opportunities.

Books on High School Internships

Following are some printed resources for learning more about internships:

✎ *The Best 109 Internships,* 9th Edition, by Mark Oldman and Samer Hamadeh.

✎ *Vault Guide to Top Internships,* 2008 Edition, by Mark Oldman.

- *Hello Real World!: A Student's Approach to Great Internships, Co-ops, and Entry-Level Positions,* by Jengyee Liang.
- *Internships (Peterson's Internships),* by Peterson's.
- *Summer Programs for Kids & Teenagers 2007,* by Peterson's.

Paid Jobs

Remember, the best jobs are usually not found online or by stopping at a local business to ask for a job. The best jobs are found through your friends, family, and network.

Still, you should read the classified ads online and in the newspaper. If you find a job you want to respond to, follow these steps:

- Print or clip out the advertisement.
- Underline the keywords and skills listed in the ad.
- Add the applicable keywords and skills to your cover letter and resume.
- Send your resume and cover letter by following the instructions in the job ad.
- Keep a copy of the ad and write on it the date you mailed your application.

Job Ad Keyword Worksheet

Find an ad for a job that sounds appealing to you. Use the following lines to list some of the keywords you can find in that ad.

_____   _____

_____   _____

_____   _____

_____   _____

Tip: The best jobs are found through your network. Talk to people that you know about your job or internship interests. Your contacts might have some ideas!

Walk-In Job Inquiries

Walking into a business or organization takes nerve, but it can result in a position. In your local area there could be businesses that are hiring full- or part-time. You never know until you ask.

How to Walk In and Ask Whether They Are Hiring

It's not always easy to just walk into a business and ask for a job. Here are some tips for how to do it:

- Have your resume ready. Look bright and friendly. Smile. Speak clearly. Look into the eyes of the first person you speak to. Look interested and serious. The hiring manager might see you right then.

- Ask who you can talk to about jobs or internships.

- Ask how you can apply for a position.

- If the company is taking applications, you can carefully fill one out while you are there or take one with you and fill it out at home.

- Ask the person who gives you the application how the hiring process works. Ask if someone will call you for an interview and how long this usually takes. Remember that the person you are talking to might say something about you to your future interviewer. If you make a good impression on that person, he or she will have good things to say, and that might get you an interview.

- Ask who the hiring manager is. Get a business card, the name of the hiring manager, and his or her e-mail address if possible.

- Ask for an appointment or the best way to communicate with that person.

- If you are given an application, attach your resume with more details of your experience. The hiring manager will be impressed with this. If you aren't given an application, ask whether you can leave a resume for the hiring manager anyway.

- If you fill out the application at home and take it back to the company later, remember that you still need to have a neat, clean appearance. You might be asked to interview right then. Be ready.

- Ask when you should call back or come back for a visit.

If you follow the preceding suggestions, the person you interact with will be impressed with your initiative and will remember you. The people you drop your application off with have lots of power when they relate their first impressions of you to their managers.

Introducing Yourself with an E-mail

Using e-mail to introduce yourself is easier than walking in the door. To introduce yourself properly by e-mail, follow these steps:

- Study your target company's Web site to find a possible contact (such as the head of engineering if you are interested in an engineering internship) and write to him or her.

- Ask whether the company is hiring high school students part-time or during summers. Also ask whether the company offers internships.

- You will probably receive a response that will be informative.

- If you do get an e-mail back and the company does hire students, e-mail your resume and cover letter for consideration or follow any application instructions you are given.

If you have skills that match the company's needs, you will probably be considered for a job or internship.

The following is an example of an e-mail you might send. In the subject line, include the name of the job or internship. Personally address the e-mail to the individual you are writing to if possible. Here's an example.

Dear Mr. Smith:

In researching companies that produce widgets, I found your Web site and would like to know whether you hire high school students part-time during the school year or full-time in the summer. I'd also like to know whether you have any internship programs.

If you do, I would appreciate your letting me know. I would like to apply for these types of positions. I am planning to pursue an engineering degree after high school, and I would like to gain experience in the business of widgets.

My skills are communication, computers (keyboard 60 wpm), and customer service.

Thanks for your help. I look forward to hearing from you.

Sincerely,

Scott Holland

Job Search Web Sites

There are many Web sites that list job openings. Start with these:

- www.craigslist.org
- www.career.com
- www.careerbuilder.com
- http://hotjobs.yahoo.com
- www.indeed.com
- www.job.com
- www.jobcentral.com
- www.monster.com
- www.nettemps.com

You can also check local newspapers' classified ads posted online.

Government and Military Web Sites

If you're looking for government or military jobs, the following are good places to start your search:

- **National Park Service** (www.nps.gov/youthprograms/): Provides information on youth programs with the National Park Service. If you enjoy the outdoors, you might look for a job as a parks worker or interpreter. Be sure you apply correctly and on time.

- **USAJOBS** (www.usajobs.gov): The official federal government job Web site.

- **STUDENTJOBS** (www.studentjobs.gov): Student page for government jobs.

- **AmeriCorps** (www.americorps.gov): Consider the AmeriCorps when you are finished with high school. You can gain great work experience and a stipend and begin your education or career. Also, your work might involve travel.

- **NASA** (www.nasajobs.nasa.gov): NASA student jobs and internships.

- **Corporation for National and Community Service** (www.nationalservice.gov): Search for interesting jobs with nonprofit and service organizations.

- **USA.gov** (www.firstgov.gov/Agencies/Federal/All_Agencies/index.shtml): If you are interested in finding internships and student job listings with a specific government agency, use this site to find the Web site for the agency's main department. Go to the agency you are seeking and look under student internships or student jobs.

- **Department of the Navy** (https://chart.donhr.navy.mil): If you live near a Navy base, it would be best to ask someone who works there for the contact information of people who could help you find a position. The Web site will not contain internships or co-op programs—only paid opportunities. You have to contact someone at the local base for internship information.

- **Civilian Personnel Online (Army)** (www.cpol.army.mil): Like the Navy, you have to find someone at your base who can help you. Find out how to contact the student recruiter who will give you information about internships, co-op programs, and entry-level positions.

> **Note**
>
> The above agency Web sites for U.S. Army and U.S. Navy civilian jobs and internships may not list actual internships for high school students, but you can learn about the Army and Navy jobs there and see the kinds of positions they are hiring for. These two Web sites have different resume builder systems for applying for jobs.

- **Air Force Personnel Center** (www.afpc.randolph.af.mil): Air Force human resources offices at each base can give you information about student hiring programs and internships. Use your network and contacts to find the information at the local base.

Interviews

So it's your big day. You have an appointment for an interview. There are several formats for interviews. Each takes certain strategies to navigate successfully. Keep the following pointers in mind.

Interview Tips for In-Person Interviews

Most interviews will be done in person. Here are some tips for doing well in them:

- Find the Web site for the company and read about its mission, customers, and focus. Be ready to answer questions about the company during the interview.

- Google the company to find other information about its services and employees, what other people have to say about it, and what's new.

- Wear an outfit that fits the company's image (no jeans). You should be dressed similarly to the way everyone else at the company dresses. If you are in doubt about how the people at the company will be dressed, dress as nicely as possible.

- Wear almost no jewelry, reasonable makeup, and a conservative hairstyle if you're a girl. If you're a boy, wear no jewelry at all and also have a conservative haircut.

- Wear very little cologne or perfume, or none at all. Some people are allergic to colognes and perfumes.

- Be confident. Remember that the company wants to hire a good employee or intern. Think positively.

- Show up a few minutes early. Don't get stressed out trying to find the location. Start early and stay calm.

- Don't be afraid to sound upbeat and hopeful for a position. It's okay to say you're good at a few things. Say a few good things about your accomplishments in school.

- Let the interviewer know why the company should hire you. Look at your resume just before you go in the door so that you will remember your skills and experience.

- Express that you would like to get experience doing this work.

- Look at chapter 2 in this book and make a list of at least five skills that you have. The interviewer might ask you what your best skills are.

- Call at least a day ahead if you need to reschedule an interview. It's okay to reschedule if something unavoidable comes up. Companies are usually accommodating if you give notice.

- Look the interviewer in the eye. Don't look down too often.

- Smile.

- Sit in a similar fashion to the interviewer. It's better to lean forward toward the interviewer.

- Breathe naturally and relax.

- Keep your resume in an attractive folder, not crumpled in your pocket or purse. Go to an office-supply store and buy a folder or notebook to hold your resume and reference sheet.

- Do not take a backpack, athletic bag, water bottle, book, or huge purse to an interview. Take only a small folder or notebook.

- Update your resume before the interview so that the interviewer does not have to ask questions that waste time.

- Bring a pen and notepad. Take a few notes during the interview. You will need these notes for writing your thank-you letter. Be sure to get the correct spelling and pronunciation of the interviewer's name and his or her title. Get a business card if you can.

- Be ready to answer questions. Also, prepare a few questions of your own while you are studying the organization's Web site. Try to ask two or three questions (other than "What does the job pay?").

- Watch your posture and don't put your hands in your pockets.

- Be yourself.

- Maintain eye contact with the interviewer when you are asked questions and are giving answers. This is very important.

- Do not speak negatively of yourself or a former employer. Skip all the bad history. For example, don't say you left your last job because the hours were too early and you're not a morning person. Do not tell the interviewer that your last supervisor was an unpleasant person (no matter how nicely you word it). Talk only about the good things. Interviewers are not impressed with anything negative. Stick with the positives about yourself and your experiences.

- Do not bring food, drink, or gum to an interview.

- Turn off your cell phone and other electronic devices, or don't bring them at all.

- Be polite. Say thank you after the interview and smile.

- It's okay to ask when the hiring manager will be making a decision about the position.

- Don't ask about salary or benefits at the first interview. Wait to see whether the interviewer is going to call you back or offer you a position. Ask about salary and benefits at that time, *before you accept the position.*

Interview Tips for Telephone Interviews

Occasionally an employer will want to interview you over the phone before meeting you—for example, if the job is far away from where you live. Here are some tips for succeeding in a phone interview:

- Schedule the time for the interview carefully so that there are no distractions and your environment will be quiet.

- Research the keywords and qualifications for the job.

- Get dressed in a good outfit so that you feel professional.

- Stand up or sit up straight during the telephone interview. Be attentive.

- Do not have the TV or music on. Do not respond to incoming calls or text messages during the interview.

- If you have your computer nearby, have the Web site of the company in front of you.

- Try to use a land line rather than a cell phone. If you use a cell phone, make sure the battery is charged and the reception is good.

- Have the job ad or internship description in front of you.

- Have the agency's mission statement in front of you.

- Have your resume in front of you.

- Listen carefully to the interviewer and take notes.

- Answer questions with a clear voice. Do not talk too fast. Be conversational, positive, and articulate.

- Don't talk too long. If your interviewer sighs or interrupts you, that is a sign that you are talking too long.

- Ask questions if you have the opportunity.

- Be friendly and enthusiastic with your voice.

- Practice a telephone interview with someone you know to get a feel for responding to questions over the phone.

- Be polite. Say thank you after the interview and smile. Even though the interviewer can't see you, she or he can "hear" your smile in your voice.

- It's okay to ask when the hiring manager will be making a decision about the position.

- Don't ask about salary or benefits at the first interview. Wait to see whether the interviewer is going to call you back or offer you a position. Ask about salary and benefits at that time, *before you accept the position*.

Accepting and Negotiating a Job or Internship Offer

Yes, a high school student can negotiate a job or internship offer. The following are some tips to keep in mind:

- When your future employer calls or writes with an offer, do *not* accept the offer immediately.

- Thank the person for the offer enthusiastically. Listen to the offer. Get information about the position. Tell this person that you would like a day to think about the position, and you will call or e-mail the next day. (Offer to e-mail only if the offer was e-mailed; otherwise, call.)

- Often the person who calls is a human resources person representing the company. This person might give you a list of benefits, hours, salary, location of the job, and when you will start. Take notes.

- You probably can negotiate salary if your qualifications are excellent or the offer is below industry standards.

- Make a list of what the company is offering. Make a list of what you want. Be reasonable.

- Call back the next day. Say that you are very pleased to be offered the position. Ask whether you can discuss the benefits, hours, and salary before making a decision.

- You will need to present your best qualifications and background to ask for an increase in the offer. If you're offered $8 per hour and you last earned $8.50, you can say this. If your last pay wasn't higher, but you feel you deserve more now, defend your position by citing your education, experience, and excellent skills.

- This is a negotiation, and you will need to be positive and persuasive. Making a list of why you believe you should earn more money is critical to success.

- Practice the negotiation.

- Ask for something different than increased pay such as training or courses that are relevant to your career field, travel or opportunities to go off-site, special projects that could be of interest to you, vacation days, or taking off a certain time (either paid or unpaid) when you have plans for a vacation or trip.

The hiring manager will think about your ideas and what you are asking for. He or she might compromise with you and raise the offer, or say that the offer cannot be changed. You will have to decide what to do. But in any event, you have discussed the salary and requested what you want. You can be proud of your efforts in discussing the position and your skills.

Sample Interview Questions for College Interviews

The following are sample questions that college recruiters and admissions interviewers might ask you, grouped by topic.

People in Your Life

- Who is someone in your life who has influenced you?

Challenges, Obstacles, and Accomplishments

- What is an obstacle that you've encountered in your life, and how have you overcome it?

- Describe an accomplishment that you've had that has shaped who you are today and how.

- What accomplishments do you feel most proud of?

- What are you looking for in a college?

- How will the colleges you have chosen to apply to help you realize the goals that you have?

- What are your goals for after high school?

Matching Your Strengths to Your Academic Disciplines

- What are your strengths outside of academics?

- How do those strengths connect with your aspirations and goals?

- Where do you want to go after receiving this degree?

About the University, College, or Internship Opportunity

- Why did you apply to this college?

- Why do you believe that this college will help your future career?

Interview Worksheet

Use the blank lines here to answer each of the questions as though you were in an interview. Practice not only answering honestly, but also answering using keywords and examples that would wow an interviewer. This exercise will help you think through effectively answering questions in any interview, whether for a college or an employment position.

Who is someone in your life who has influenced you?

_____

_____

What is an obstacle that you've encountered in your life, and how have you overcome it?

_____

_____

_____

Describe an accomplishment that you've had that has shaped who you are today and how.

_____

_____

_____

What accomplishments do you feel most proud of?

_____

_____

What are you looking for in a college/employer?

_____

_____

How will the colleges/companies you have chosen to apply to help you realize the goals that you have?

_____

_____

What are your goals for after high school?

_____

_____

What are your strengths outside of academics?

_____

_____

How do those strengths connect with your aspirations and goals?

_____

_____

_____

(continued)

(continued)

Where do you want to go after receiving this degree?

_____

_____

_____

Why did you apply to this college/company?

_____

_____

_____

Why do you believe that this college will help your future career?

_____

_____

_____

What's Next?

In this chapter, you learned how to search for and apply to jobs and internships, as well as interview for admission to colleges and other academic and training programs. You can take everything you've learned in this book about preparing your high school resume and use it to further your career and your education. We wish you much success!

Index

X–Z